TEACH YOURSELF BOOKS

BRIDGE

Terence Reese

NTC *NTC Publishing Group*

795.4
Ree
a.93

Long-renowned as *the* authoritative source for self-guided
learning – with more than 30 million copies sold worldwide –
the *Teach Yourself* series includes over 200 titles in the fields
of languages, crafts, hobbies, sports, and other leisure activities.

This edition was first published in 1992 by NTC Publishing Group,
4255 West Touhy Avenue, Lincolnwood (Chicago), Illinois 60646 –
1975 U.S.A. Originally published by Hodder and Stoughton Ltd.
Copyright 1980 by Terrence Reese.

Library of Congress Catalog Card Number 92–80866

Printed in England by Clays Ltd, St Ives plc.

Contents

Foreword		vi
1	If you are a Real Beginner	1
2	Making Tricks in a Single Suit	17
3	The Play at Notrumps	28
4	Opening 1NT and Responses	35
5	The Play in a Suit Contract	42
6	Opening Suit Bids of One and Responses	52
7	The Second Round	68
8	The Strong Openings – 2NT, Two of a Suit, Two Clubs	79
9	Opening Bids of Three and Four	84
10	Slam Bidding	89
11	The Scoring	94
12	Defensive Overcalls	97
13	Penalty and Take-out Doubles	103
14	Stratagems in Play	114
15	Leads and Signals	121
Glossary of Bridge Terms and Phrases		129
Index		137

Foreword

Bridge is not the easiest of games to learn, but of all leisure pastimes it is possibly the most rewarding. You will have a hobby that never palls and a sure way of making friends wherever you go.

Mindful of the title of this series, I have started on the assumption that the reader may know nothing whatsoever about the game. The pace is stepped up later, but I have aimed always to carry the reader with me. Some books rove from the simplest instruction to chapters on relatively advanced subjects, such as squeeze play. I have always thought it silly, unless you are writing a 500-page textbook, to include subjects that normally are spanned by an interval of five years' experience.

A small problem, always, is the degree of attention to be paid to the numerous differences in bidding style – weak or strong notrump, for example. In earlier books I have usually described just one style, for simplicity. This time, however, I have commented on variations in practice and have given a brief account of some popular conventions. You will need to know about such matters when, as I hope you will, you move into higher spheres. The greatest pleasure in Bridge comes from trying to improve, so treat the game as a challenge, not just as a recreation.

Terence Reese

I

If You are a Real Beginner

So, what *do* you know about this game?

That it is a game for four players, two on each side, the partners facing one another?

That it is played with a normal pack of fifty-two cards (with the jokers removed from a new pack)?

That people seem to go mad about the game, that your cousin Mary says you simply must learn, but she hasn't time to teach you, can't you just pick it up by watching?

This last suggestion contains only a partial truth. There is a limit to what you can learn entirely on your own, just as there is a limit to the skill you could acquire at golf by learning to swing indoors. On the other hand, a little intelligent practice before you try to hit a golf ball on the course will enable you to learn the game far more quickly. It is the same in Bridge.

Take thirteen cards only

To make a start, I want you first to pick out thirteen cards of a suit – say, spades. These cards have a ranking order, as follows:

A K Q J 10 (called *Honours*)*

9 8 7 6 5 4 3 2

Not difficult to remember. Ace counts high, King (*pace* the feminists) ranks above the Queen, Jack (also called Knave) is

---

* Most words that have a special meaning in Bridge, when used for the first time, are printed in italics.

evidently inferior, and the rest are in numerical order. The distinction between honour cards and plain cards is not important. The top cards possess no special magic in the play, but in certain circumstances you may score a bonus for holding four or five honours in the same suit or for possessing four Aces.

The play at Bridge consists of a series of *tricks*. Each player is dealt thirteen cards and contributes one card to each of thirteen tricks. If possible, he must play a card of the suit led.

You have extracted the thirteen spades from the pack. Let us look at the play of some tricks in which a spade has been led.

♠ 5

♠ 8 (led)   N W E S   ♠ Q

♠ A

The N S W and E signs are a purely literary device to indicate the relative positions of the players. North and South are partners against East and West. These terms are not used at the table, except in tournament play.

West has led the 8 of spades. Then, in clockwise order, North has played the 5, East the Queen, and South the Ace. Whose trick? South's, because he has played the highest spade – the Ace. Having won the trick, South would lead. The next trick goes:

♠ 3

♠ 2   N W E S   ♠ 4

♠ J (led)

South has led the Jack of spades and this has won the trick. Somebody (perhaps South himself) must hold the King, a higher card, but it is by no means always correct to play your highest card, even when it might win the trick.

By this time eight cards have been played in spades, and the next time spades are led, at least one player might hold no more. This brings us to a new situation.

The effect of discards

When a player is unable to follow suit, because he holds no more cards of the suit led, he is said to *discard*. Except in the special circumstances described in the next section a card from a different suit has no power to win the trick. Forgetting about the spades played in the examples above, suppose that a trick were to go like this:

♠ 5 (led)

♠ 7   [N W E S box]   ♦ 10

♠ 9

North has led 5 of spades, East has discarded the 10 of diamonds, and South's 9 of spades wins the trick. This type of situation may well arise towards the end of a hand:

♡ 9

♣ 8   [N W E S box]   ♡10

♠ 3 (led)

South leads the 3 of spades. As no-one is able to follow suit, the lowly 3 wins the trick.

The factor of trumps

You have heard about *trumps*, no doubt. In Bridge some hands – not all, but the majority – are played with one suit designated as trumps. The effect of this is that a card of the trump suit has power to win the trick over any card of another suit. When there is a trump suit, the other suits are referred to as *plain* suits or *side* suits. But the obligation to follow suit remains. Unless it is your turn to lead, you may play a trump only if unable to play a card of the suit led. In this example clubs are trumps:

♠ 8

♡ 4 (led)

N
W   E
S

♣ 2

♡ K

West leads a low heart. North, having no hearts, and not wishing to play a trump (or perhaps not holding a trump) discards a spade. East plays a trump, the 2 of clubs. This is usually described as *ruffing*. South's heart King is the highest card of the suit led, but East has won the trick and will lead to the next trick. Another example, again with clubs as trumps:

◇ 10 (led)

♣ 9

N
W   E
S

◇ Q

♣ 5

North's lead of the 10 of diamonds is covered by the Queen, and so far it is East's trick. But South ruffs and West, also unable to follow suit, *overruffs*. It is West's trick.

How the trump suit is determined

Which suit, if any, shall be trumps is determined by the *bidding*. In practice, the bidding precedes the play, but I have described what happens in the play first, because otherwise the bidding process would be meaningless.

You will find it easy to understand, I am sure, that to choose a trump suit that fits your hand is an important objective. To give a slightly exaggerated example, suppose you held in spades this suit:

♠ K Q J 10 8 7 6 4

With spades as trumps you would hold, in Bridge idiom, seven solid tricks. You have eight spades and, once the Ace has been forced out, the remaining seven will be 'good' (barring an extremely bad division, one opponent holding all five outstanding cards). But if the hand were played with another suit as trumps, or with no suit as trumps, the spades might bring in no tricks at all.

Consequently, the general object of bidding is to establish a favourable trump suit. Bidding takes the form of an auction, the player who makes the highest bid obtaining the *contract*, presumably one that favours his side. We look next at the procedure in bidding.

The bidding process

First, the suits, and the denomination of *Notrumps*, have a ranking order:

> Notrumps
> Spades
> Hearts
> Diamonds
> Clubs

Spades and hearts are *major* suits, diamonds and clubs are *minor* suits. The significance of the ranking order is that a contract to win, say, ten tricks out of thirteen, with spades as trumps, outranks a contract to win the same number of tricks with hearts as trumps.

In naming a bid there is what you may think of as a verbal peculiarity. First, you must contract to win at least seven tricks, and this is expressed not by bidding, say, Seven Clubs, but by bidding One Club. In other words, you undertake, when you bid One Club, to take the odd trick (seven out of thirteen) with clubs as trumps. One Club is the lowest possible bid, and Seven No-trumps, which can be written as 7NT, is the highest.

There are two other important features of bidding that you need to understand before we look at examples. First, you are never under a 'legal' obligation to make a bid: you may always *pass*, which at the table is generally signified by the spoken words, *No Bid*. Occasionally, all four players will pass. This is called a *throw-in*: the deal then passes to the next player. Second, just as in a commercial auction you have to consider the amount of money you will be required to pay for your choice, so in bidding you must take into account that if you fail in the contract you have named you will lose a *penalty*. Furthermore, the opponents, if they think you have gone too far, may *double*, greatly increasing the penalties. Finally, if you think in turn that the opponents are wrong and that you will make your contract, you may *redouble*, again raising the stakes.*

You are ready now to look at some typical bidding sequences. If South has dealt the cards, he will make the first *call*. A call is a comprehensive term, covering any bid, pass, double or re-double.

South	West	North	East
No	1H	2C	2H
No	No	No	

South, the dealer, lacking the values for an opening bid, passes. This is sometimes written as 'pass', sometimes as 'No', short for No Bid.

West is strong enough to open the bidding. His bid of One Heart, remember, is nominally an undertaking to win seven tricks with hearts as trumps – seven tricks, that is, with the aid of his partner's hand. However, he does not have this principally in mind when he opens the bidding. He is saying, 'I have a hand of certain strength and one of my suits, probably my main suit, is hearts.'

---

* To prevent later confusion, it may be said now that these calls, double and redouble, do not always bear their natural meaning. Double, especially, often carries a different message.

The next opponent, North, has a suit of clubs and sufficient strength for an *overcall* of Two Clubs, which in theory amounts to an undertaking to make eight tricks with clubs as trumps.

East, bidding Two Hearts, *supports*, or *raises*, his partner. As we shall discover later, this is a comparatively weak bid. South has nothing to say, and West, despite the support from his partner, does not aspire to a higher contract. North passes, too, and there the bidding ends.

Now an auction that contains a double:

South	West	North	East
1H	1S	3H	3S
4H	4S	dble	No
No	No		

South opens One Heart and West overcalls with One Spade. North, with support for his partner's suit, jumps to Three Hearts, and East in turn raises his partner to Three Spades.

Encouraged by his partner's raise, South goes to Four Hearts, which, as we shall see in the next section, represents an important stage. However, West does not give in. He may not be confident of making Four Spades, but he is willing to concede a small penalty to prevent the opponents from scoring well in their contract. This is (presumably) a *save* or *sacrifice*. North decides to double Four Spades in preference to attempting Five Hearts.

We remarked above that Four Hearts represented an important stage in bidding. It is time now to examine what that means.

Part score, game, slam, and rubber

The five denominations that we noted at the beginning of the previous section have certain values in the scoring.

The first trick in a notrump contract counts 40, all subsequent tricks, 30.

Each trick in a major suit (spades or hearts) counts 30.

Each trick in a minor suit (diamonds or clubs) counts 20.

A primary objective in bidding is to score *game*. The first side to score two games wins the *rubber*, which carries a considerable bonus. To make a game, you need a trick score of 100 or more.

Thus game can be made from a love score by way of any of these contracts:

> 3NT (40 + 30 + 30)
> Four Hearts or Four Spades (4 × 30)
> Five Clubs or Five Diamonds (5 × 20)

Lesser contracts are described as *part scores*. It is possible to score game by making two or more part scores whose trick score totals 100. If you make, say, Two Spades on the first hand of a rubber, and Three Diamonds on a later hand, that will be enough for game, provided that neither side has made a game contract in the meanwhile. Thus, if you make Two Spades on the first hand but the opponents then make game with 3NT, your part score of Two Spades, worth 60, is cancelled to the extent that it will not contribute to a future game.

Special bonuses are scored for *slam* contracts. A contract to make twelve tricks – 6NT, for example – is a *small slam*, a contract to make all thirteen tricks a *grand slam*.

A doubled part-score contract may produce a game. Say that the bidding goes:

South	West	North	East
1NT	2S	dble	No
No	No		

Here West has overcalled 1NT with Two Spades and North, taking into account his partner's opening bid, doubles. This does not raise the level of the contract: either East, South or West could remove the double by making a higher bid, such as Three Clubs. However, all pass, and West will attempt to make Two Spades doubled. If he succeeds, he will score 120, enough for game, plus a small bonus for making a doubled contract. To make Three Spades doubled would also produce a game, obviously, but would not count as a slam.

Declarer and dummy

There is one further important feature we have not mentioned. When the final contract has been determined, the player who first named the denomination of this contract is called the *declarer*. The player on his left makes the *opening lead*, and the declarer's partner lays down his cards. This player, and the hand he exposes, are both referred to as *dummy*. The declarer now plays the cards from both hands. Dummy has certain limited rights but may not advise the declarer in any way.

This exposing of the dummy hand, in case you are interested, is one of the distinguishing features between Bridge and the older game of Whist. Also, in Whist there is no bidding – the trump suit is determined by turning up a card. The difference between Auction Bridge and the modern game of Contract, now simply called Bridge, is that in Auction you would not have to bid game or slam to score the appropriate bonus. You could play in One Spade, and if you made enough tricks you would be credited with the bonuses for game or slam.

You play your first hand

By this time, like the golfer who wants to go out on the course, you may feel that you would like to play a complete hand. We will start from the point at which four players decide to make up a game. First, unless the partnerships are prearranged, they *cut for partners*. A pack is spread face down and each player withdraws a card. The players drawing the highest cards, in a Bridge sense, are partners against the other two. Thus suppose the cards drawn are S J, H 6, D 6 and C 4. The players with S J and H 6 have choice of seats and cards. (It is usual to play with two packs, which are used for alternate deals.) The player who drew S J elects to sit South and we will say that he chooses the blue pack. This is shuffled by West, then passed to East, who cuts the pack into two parts. South completes the cut, then deals the first card to West, the next to North, and so on. He will deal the last card, the fifty-second, to himself. Otherwise, it would be a *misdeal*.

When the deal has been completed, the four players pick up their hands and sort them into suits. This is the full hand:

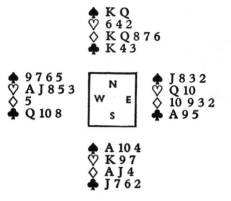

The dealer, South, makes the first call. Having a fairly balanced hand that is better than average, he opens 1NT. West has a suit of hearts, but it would be dangerous to overcall, so he passes. North raises to 3NT, a game bid. He does not mention his diamonds, because to make game in diamonds his side would need to make eleven tricks, while only nine tricks are needed for game at notrumps. The others all pass, and this ends the bidding, which would be represented as follows:

South	West	North	East
1NT	No	3NT	No
No	No		

Before we study the play in 3NT, let me say a word about Bridge diagrams. If you can 'read' the diagram above, so much the better. If you find such a diagram confusing, then pick out all the cards and play through the deal, card by card. Try, however, to familiarise yourself with the written diagram, as you will then make faster progress. Within a short while a diagram of fifty-two cards will be as easy to read as a price list – and less painful.

Since South is the player who first mentioned the denomination in which the hand is to be played, he is the declarer, and West, the player on his left, makes the opening lead. Following general principles when *defending* against notrumps, West would lead from his longest suit, and the natural choice here would be the fourth best card, the 5. (This is better than leading the Ace.)

When West's lead has been placed in the middle of the table, North lays down his dummy. It is usual to display the dummy vertically, rather than horizontally, as in a written diagram. So North will lay down his cards in this way:

There is no prescribed order of suits when laying down the dummy in a notrump contract, but it is usual to alternate the red and black suits, as has been done here.

Remember, now, that South, the declarer, plays the cards from both hands. Before playing to the first trick, it is sensible to form a general plan. Bear in mind, first, that you are playing 3NT and that your object is to make nine tricks. To make extra tricks, called *overtricks*, is unimportant, although each overtrick adds to the score.

This is an easy hand to play, but we will take it trick by trick.

Trick 1

West's lead of the 5 of hearts is covered by the 2, Queen and King. The lead has not worked out well for the defence, because it has allowed South to make a trick with the King of hearts. South gathers the four cards played and lays them face down.

Trick 2

Counting his tricks, South sees that he has a good chance to make five in diamonds, three in spades, and one in hearts, which will be enough for game. First, he lays down the Ace of diamonds. When all follow, the contract is assured. The other hands all play low on the Ace of diamonds. South places this trick neatly across the first trick.

Trick 3
South *could* make a horrible error at this point. If he were to follow with the Jack of diamonds he might never make the three tricks that are available in spades. (After running the diamonds and cashing the King, Queen of Spades, he would not be able to return to his hand to make the Ace of spades.) His next move must be a low spade to dummy's Queen. Again, the defenders play low.

Trick 4
Following his plan, South cashes dummy's King of spades.

Trick 5
He returns a low diamond to the Jack. West, having no more diamonds, discards a spade.

Trick 6
Before leaving his hand, South is careful to cash the Ace of spades.

Tricks 7 to 9
South makes three more tricks in diamonds.

The declarer has made his contract now. He would not play out the remainder of the hand, but would concede the last four tricks. (South could, in fact, have claimed nine tricks as soon as everyone followed to the Ace of diamonds, and in a moderately advanced game he would probably do so.)

The second pack, the red pack, would have been shuffled, or *made*, by North while South was dealing the first hand. When the cards from this first deal have been collected (by East), the second pack would be passed to South, to cut for the next deal.

You play your second hand

While West is dealing the second hand of the rubber, East shuffles the other pack and lays it down on his right. The cards fall in this way:

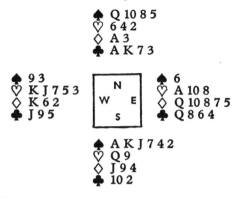

```
              ♠ Q 10 8 5
              ♡ 6 4 2
              ◇ A 3
              ♣ A K 7 3

♠ 9 3                           ♠ 6
♡ K J 7 5 3      ┌─────────┐    ♡ A 10 8
◇ K 6 2          │    N    │    ◇ Q 10 8 7 5
♣ J 9 5          │ W     E │    ♣ Q 8 6 4
                 │    S    │
                 └─────────┘
              ♠ A K J 7 4 2
              ♡ Q 9
              ◇ J 9 4
              ♣ 10 2
```

The bidding goes:

South	West	North	East
—	No	1C	No
1S	No	2S	No
4S	No	No	No

South, whose hand contains several *losers* in the side suits, is not confident that he will make Four Spades, but it is natural for him to attempt a game contract. If South bid only Three Spades, North might go to Four.

Trick 1
West has no very attractive lead. Let us say that he begins with the 5 of hearts. When laying down the dummy in a trump contract it is correct always to place trumps on the right. So North puts down the spades first. Declarer plays low from dummy and East wins with the Ace of hearts.

Trick 2
East returns the 10 of hearts, which is covered by the Queen and King.

Trick 3
Though he does not expect it to win, West continues with the Jack of hearts.

Having no more hearts, South is able to ruff this trick with a low spade. Dummy at this point may say, 'Having none?' This warns declarer not to *revoke*, an offence that incurs a heavy penalty.

Tricks 4 and 5

South draws two rounds of trumps with the Ace and King. Unless there is a reason to do otherwise, it is wise to draw trumps as soon as possible.

South's two club losers are covered by dummy's Ace and King. He has two diamond losers on the surface, but after he has lost the second round he can ruff the third round with a trump in dummy. He could, in fact, lay down his cards at this point, claiming ten tricks.

This deal illustrates two important advantages that may arise from playing in a suit contract. First, South was able to arrest the run of the hearts by ruffing the third round. Had he been playing in 3NT he would have lost the first five tricks after a heart lead. Second, South was able to ruff the third round of diamonds in dummy. This in effect extended the trick-winning power of the trump suit. The declarer made the six trumps in his own hand, plus an extra trick in dummy.

About the scoring

You have made two game contracts, one in 3NT, one in Four Spades, so you have won the rubber. You will have scored 920 points altogether – 100 for 3NT, 120 for Four Spades, and 700 for a rubber won in two games. If you had won the rubber by the odd game in three, the bonus would be only 500.

There is a chapter on scoring much later in the book (see p. 94). For the moment I do not propose to go into the details. With no point of reference you would find the scores difficult to remember. When you have played a little, scoring is no problem, because the same situations constantly recur.

All that I want you to understand now is that a line is drawn across the centre of the scoresheet and that scores for tricks made (such as 100 for 3NT) are entered *below the line* and all other scores, such as penalties and bonuses, *above the line*. Suppose, for example, that you bid Two Hearts and make nine tricks in the play. You enter just 60 below the line, 30 above for the overtrick. Thus you have a part score of 60. If you could make, say, 1NT on a subsequent hand, that would be enough for game, provided always that neither side had scored a game in the meantime.

And one other feature of the scoring must be mentioned. When you have made a game you become *vulnerable*. Penalties are now much increased.

Progress review

A lot of ground has been covered in this chapter. See if you can answer the following questions:

1 Who deals the first hand of a rubber?
2 If East is dealing with the red pack, who will shuffle the blue pack?
3 How many tricks are required for game in hearts?
4 How many tricks are required for game in clubs?
5 What happens if everyone passes?
6 Which player makes the opening lead?
7 At what point is the dummy exposed?
8 In a trump contract, where does dummy place the trump suit?
9 What is meant by discarding?
10 What is meant by ruffing?
11 What would you score for 2NT, making Four?
12 What would you score for Four Spades, making Six?

Answers
1 The player who drew the highest card in the cut for partners.
2 His partner, West, ready for South to deal the next hand.
3 Ten – a trick score of 120.
4 Eleven – a trick score of 100.
5 The deal passes to the next player.
6 The player on the left of the declarer.
7 After the opening lead has been placed on the table.

8 On the right.

9 Playing a card (not a trump) of a suit other than the one led.

10 Playing a trump on the lead of a plain suit.

11 70 below, 60 above. (Remember that the first trick in no-trumps counts 40.)

12 Strictly, 120 below and 60 above, but since game has been made, there is no objection to entering 180 below, and this is normally done. Remember that you do not score the slam bonus unless you bid the slam.

2

Making Tricks in a Single Suit

Although, as you well understand by now, bidding precedes play, I still think we would do better to examine simple ideas in play before we study the technique of bidding. Until you have a rough idea of how tricks are won and plans are formed, you won't understand why, for example, it is reasonable to contract for 3NT on two hands in combination. First, we are going to look at ways of establishing tricks in a single suit. It is essential to be able to recognise at once how many tricks you can expect to make from a particular suit. It is not difficult to judge that when you hold, say, A x x opposite K Q x (the x standing for any low card) you can make three tricks. But that is only a beginning: there are numerous other ways of establishing tricks from less substantial holdings.

Forcing out defensive winners

Suppose, first, that the important card you are missing is the Ace. This is the simplest holding:

North
Q J 5

South
K 7 4

So long as you do not commit the folly of playing two high cards on the same trick, you can be sure of two tricks. You can play a low card to the Queen and, if the Ace does not appear, the 5 back to the King. You are certain to win two tricks.

The play here is much the same:

North
Q J 10 5

South
K 4

By leading the King, and following with the 4, you can establish three winners. Note that it is normally advisable to start with the high card from the shorter hand. In the present example, if you began by playing the Queen from dummy and followed with the 5 to the King, the opponents might decline to part with the Ace. You would then need two *entry cards* to dummy to force out the Ace and win the remaining trick.

We turn next to combinations where you need to force out more than one high card.

North
Q 10 8 5

South
J 9 2

After the defenders have taken the Ace and King you will win two tricks.

North
J 9 7 4 3

South
10 8

Given time, and sufficient entries to the North hand, you will be able to establish two winners after forcing out the Ace, King and Queen.

Leading towards high cards

Very often, your chances of developing extra tricks will depend on the position of the adverse cards. The general principle is to lead *towards*, not away from, high-card combinations that are not *solid*. This is the simplest example:

North
K 4

South
6 5 2

Leading from the South hand, you will make a trick with the King whenever the Ace is held by West. If you arrive at a position where you have to lead from North, you will never make your King.

North
Q 6 3

South
A 7 2

To make two tricks from this combination, you must lead from the South hand, hoping that the King is held by West. It is useless to lead the Queen from dummy, for if East has the King he will (or normally should) cover the Queen. It is the same when you are missing both Ace and King.

North
Q J 6

West   *East*
A 5 2   K 10 8 3

South
9 7 4

You can establish a trick only if you lead twice from your hand.

Establishing low-card winners

It may surprise you to learn that nearly half the tricks in an average deal are won not by honour cards, but by low cards. You will soon find it quite easy to assess the prospects of establishing low-card winners.

North
A Q 5

South
K 8 6 3

You start with three guaranteed winners. What about the fourth round? If the suit is divided 3–3, your fourth card (at notrumps, anyway) will take the last trick. The odds are some-what against a 3–3 division, but the chance is by no means negligible.

North
A 8 6 4 2

South
K Q 3

Now you have a good chance to develop five tricks. There are only five of the suit against you and they are likely to break 3–2. If they are 4–1, then you may have time to establish the fifth round after conceding one trick to the opposition.

This last example brings us to a new idea: very often, on the way to establishing low-card winners, you will need to surrender one or more tricks to the opponents.

North
A 5 2

South
K 8 6 3

This is the same combination as the first in this section, except that you no longer hold the Queen. However, you have the same chance as before of establishing a low-card winner. In a notrump contract you would probably give up a trick early on, retaining control. If the suit breaks 3–3, you will make a third trick in due course.

North
4

South
A K Q 7 5 2

This suit may develop six tricks. A 4–2 break is rather more likely, but you will still make five tricks, after losing one.

In this next example you combine the technique of promoting high cards and establishing low ones:

North
K Q 7 5 2

West
A 10 4

East
J 9

South
8 6 3

When you make the first lead towards dummy, West will probably play low. The King wins and you must return to hand for the next lead. With the cards lying favourably, you can develop four tricks.

The simple finesse

One of the commonest manoeuvres in play is the *finesse*. This is an attempt to win a trick owing to the favourable position of an adverse honour. Finesses against the King, Queen, Jack, and 10 are almost equally common, and towards the end of the play a finesse may be taken against much lower cards.

North
A Q 5

West   *East*
K 8 3   9 7 4 2

South
J 10 6

South would approach this suit by leading the Jack or 10 from his hand. Whether or not West covers on the first round, three tricks are assured.

North
A 5 2

West   *East*
10 7 4   Q 9 3

South
K J 8 6

By playing the Ace, then finessing the Jack and laying down the King, South can make four tricks. Transfer the Queen to West, and he would make only two tricks unless he could persuade West to open the suit.

North
K 10 5

West   *East*
J 8 4   A 7 3

South
Q 9 6 2

The important card here is the Jack. South has what is called a two-way finesse, because he can play either opponent for the critical card. It is normally convenient to finesse first in the shorter of the two hands, and this method works well in the present situation. If South begins with a finesse of the 10 he can make three tricks.

```
              North
              Q 9 4
      West              East
      K 10 3            A 8
              South
              J 7 6 5 2
```

South begins by leading low towards the dummy. When West plays low, he finesses the 9. As the cards lie, he can develop three tricks.

Double and combination finesses

When you need to find two cards, or one of two cards, favourably placed, you are said to take a double or combination finesse. Missing the King and Jack in this example, you have a chance for a double finesse:

```
              North
              7 4 2

              South
              A Q 10
```

You begin by leading from dummy and finessing the 10. If this wins, you finesse the Queen on the next round, making three tricks if East began with K J x.

```
              North
              K J 9 5
      West              East
      Q 10 6            A 8 2
              South
              7 4 3
```

Owing to the favourable lie, you can make three tricks if you begin with a finesse of the 9.

When two cards of equal rank are missing, you take a combination finesse. This is a very common situation:

North
A J 10 7 4

West   *East*
K 9 2   Q 8

South
6 5 3

You play for the honours to be divided. A finesse of the 10 loses to the Queen, but a finesse of the Jack on the next round brings in the rest of the tricks. It is true that if East held K Q alone this would not be the best line of play, but except in special circumstances (East being marked with strength) the combination finesse would offer a much better chance.

North
8 5 3 2

West   *East*
A J 4   Q 7 6

South
K 10 9

You begin by leading from dummy and finessing the 10, which loses to the Jack. On the next round finesse the 9. This, in principle, is better than playing the King, though again there may be special circumstances.

A combination finesse against the J 10 will gain a trick less often, but it is the right play with this kind of combination:

North
A Q 9 6 2

West   *East*
J 10 4   K 8

South
7 5 3

Attempting to develop four tricks, it costs nothing to finesse the 9 on the first round. Clearly, if you play the Queen first time, you will lose two tricks instead of one. Finessing the 9 makes no difference when West has, say, K 10 4 and East J 8. After the 9 has lost to the Jack, you can finesse the Queen on the next round.

When a finesse may be the wrong play

Do you remember this combination from the section 'leading towards high cards' above (p. 18)?

North
Q 6 3

South
A 7 2

The best chance, it was said, for two tricks was to lead to-wards the Queen. To lead the Queen from dummy would be a mistake, because East, with K x or K 10 x or any similar holding, would cover the Queen with the King. Thus you would lose the chance of finding the King with West. This is another holding of the same type:

North
J 7 2

South
A K 6 5

To lead the Jack from dummy could hardly gain. The best chance for three tricks is to lead low from hand. This works well when West holds Q 10 x x or a *doubleton* Q x. It is true that to play off the Ace and King would be better if East held Q x, but this line would fail when East held any other doubleton.

If you add the 10 to the South hand, a finesse is playable, but it is important now to lead *low* from the North hand.

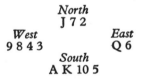

North
J 7 2

West
9 8 4 3

East
Q 6

South
A K 10 5

Do you see that it would be a mistake to lead the Jack from dummy? East would cover with the Queen and West would win the fourth round. The right play is to lead the 2 from North and finesse the 10.

The best play with this type of holding depends very much on the circumstances:

North
A J 6 3

South
Q 5

If you were playing in a suit contract, with plenty of trumps in your hand, you would probably seek two *immediate* tricks by leading the Queen and finessing. You might then lose no tricks at all in the suit. But in a notrump contract, if your object was to make three tricks, it would be better to lead low from dummy towards the Q x. The distribution might be:

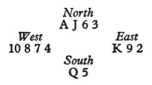

On the lead of the 3 East may go up with the King. You then have three easy tricks. If East plays low, the Queen wins and your best plan is to *duck* on the way back, playing the 6 from dummy. On the next round the Ace will bring down the King.

There is often a choice between taking a finesse and playing for the *drop*. You will encounter this situation many thousands of times in your Bridge career:

North
A 8 4 2

South
K J 7 5 3

You lead the Ace from dummy and follow with the 2. Assuming that the Queen has not appeared, the mathematical odds, with nine cards, slightly favour playing for the drop of the Queen. However, tactical considerations often point to a finesse. With eight cards instead of nine, in a similar situation, the finesse is the better chance for five tricks.

Exercises in the play of a single suit

In the questions that follow, a number of unfamiliar combinations will occur, so don't be depressed if you don't get all the answers right. It is still a most valuable exercise to work out the possibilities.

In each case attempt to answer three questions:

(a) What is the fewest number of tricks you can be sure of making?

(b) What is the greatest number of tricks you can hope to make?

(c) How would you play for the maximum?

1 K Q J 5	**2** A J 7 5 3
7 4 2	Q 6 4
3 A 7 5	**4** K Q 6 4 2
Q J 4 3	8 5
5 Q 10 7 4 2	**6** A J 9 5 4
A 5 3	6 3

Answers

1 (a) Fewest number – 2.

  (b) Greatest number – 3.

  (c) Best play – lead each time from the South hand until the Ace has appeared. This way, you make three tricks when West holds A x or A 10 x x, as well as when the suit breaks 3–3.

2 (a) The practical answer is three, though this might be difficult if all five outstanding cards were in one hand.

  (b) You could make all five tricks if West held K x.

  (c) Begin with a low card to the Jack.

3 (a) Two.

  (b) Three.

  (c) Lead low from dummy towards the Q J x x. This way, you make three tricks when East holds K x or K 10 x x as well as when the suit breaks 3–3.

4 (a) One – if East held A J 10 9 x over the dummy.

  (b) Four.

  (c) Lead twice toward the dummy, playing West for A x x.

5 (a) One.

  (b) Four.

  (c) Lead the Ace and follow with a finesse of the 10. You will develop four tricks when East holds K x or K x x, and also when West holds K J x x. It is because of this last possibility that a finesse of the 10 is mathematically better than going up with the Queen (which would be best if West held K x x and East J x).

6 (a) One.

  (b) Four.

  (c) The best chance is to finesse the 9 on the first round, with a second finesse in reserve should the 9 be captured by the King or Queen. You are playing for West to hold K 10 x or Q 10 x.

3

The Play at Notrumps

Let us see now if you can 'put it together'. You have learned how to estimate the number of tricks that can be developed from various suit combinations. In this chapter you play four hands in 3NT, so in each case you will need to make nine tricks. At the beginning of the play – as soon as the dummy goes down – form a plan. Count the certain winners and then consider how you can develop the extra tricks needed for your contract.

Establishing the longest suit

The play at notrumps often develops into a race between the two sides to establish their respective long suits. The opening leader will usually begin with his longest suit, and the declarer will usually begin, not necessarily with his longest suit, but with the suit that is capable of developing the greatest number of extra tricks.

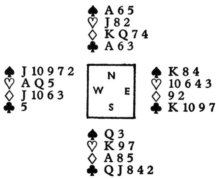

```
              ♠ A 6 5
              ♡ J 8 2
              ◇ K Q 7 4
              ♣ A 6 3
♠ J 10 9 7 2    ┌─────────┐    ♠ K 8 4
♡ A Q 5         │    N    │    ♡ 10 6 4 3
◇ J 10 6 3    W │         │ E  ◇ 9 2
♣ 5             │    S    │    ♣ K 10 9 7
              └─────────┘
              ♠ Q 3
              ♡ K 9 7
              ◇ A 8 5
              ♣ Q J 8 4 2
```

If you have a problem in reading the diagram, lay out the cards and follow the play in 3NT trick by trick.

Trick 1
West leads the Jack of spades. This is top of a *sequence* (J 10 9) in his longest suit. South plays low from dummy and the King wins.

Trick 2
East returns his partner's suit, leading the 8 of spades to South's Queen.

Trick 3
South could cash three top diamonds, with a chance of making the 'long' diamond, the thirteenth, but this would be poor play. Instead, he should aim to develop four tricks in clubs. The best way to do this is not to finesse the Queen, but to play low to the Ace.

Trick 4
A low club is led from dummy. East might go up with the King, but we will say that he plays low, making it more difficult for South to establish the suit. South wins with the Queen. West discards the 5 of hearts.

Trick 5
Knowing that East still holds C K 10, South crosses to the King of diamonds for the next lead of clubs.

Trick 6
Declarer leads a club from dummy and now East plays the King. Realising that he must keep all his diamonds, and hoping that his partner will now *clear* the spades by playing a third round, West discards the Queen of hearts.

South has nine tricks on top now (two in spades, three in diamonds and four in clubs). He may, in practice, make a tenth trick because West will be embarrassed by further club leads.

Note that South would probably have failed in his contract if he had tested the diamonds before playing on clubs. He would have set up a diamond winner for West. When East came in with the King of clubs, West would discard a spade and East would lead a heart. West would then make two hearts and a diamond, giving the defence five tricks.

Playing for two chances

A declarer will often be able to test his luck in two suits. Observe how the chances are combined in this deal:

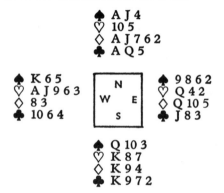

♠ A J 4
♡ 10 5
◇ A J 7 6 2
♣ A Q 5

♠ K 6 5
♡ A J 9 6 3
◇ 8 3
♣ 10 6 4

♠ 9 8 6 2
♡ Q 4 2
◇ Q 10 5
♣ J 8 3

♠ Q 10 3
♡ K 8 7
◇ K 9 4
♣ K 9 7 2

Again the contract is 3NT by South.

Trick 1

West leads the 6 of hearts – fourth best from his longest suit. East plays the Queen and South wins with the King.

The best play on this hand requires a little thought. Five tricks in diamonds, or even four tricks, would bring in the game easily, but there is an obvious danger in finessing the Jack. If the finesse loses, the defenders will almost surely be able to cash four winners in hearts.

Looking at other possibilities, South observes that a successful finesse in spades will also produce enough tricks for game – three spades, one heart, two diamonds, and at least three clubs.

There is a simple way to combine the chances. Begin by playing off Ace and King of diamonds. If the Queen does not fall, you can turn to spades. You are giving up the best chance in diamonds, but only to a small degree. So the play continues:

Trick 2
King of diamonds.

Trick 3
A diamond to the Ace. The Queen is still against you.

Tricks 4 to 6
Since the contract is going to depend now on the spade finesse, and you will certainly be defeated if this loses, there is no great harm – also no great advantage – in playing off the top clubs.

Trick 7
As everyone has followed to three rounds of clubs, you are able to cash the last club. Both defenders discard a spade.

Digressing for a moment, do not, even as a beginner, form the habit of counting the cards in each suit as it is played. That is to say, when three rounds of clubs have been played and everyone has followed suit, you should know without counting that the last club is good. If you need to count on every occasion, you will be like a typist who has to look at the keys. You must reserve your concentration for more important matters and aim to acquire a sense of the unchanging suit distributions. No matter if at first you make an occasional mistake. The only time when it may be necessary to count the cards that have been played in a suit is when you are playing off a long suit and the opponents have to make several discards.

Returning to the present deal, after you have cashed the long club, you run the 10 of spades. The finesse wins and you end up with ten tricks.

When the long suit is not safe

This is another deal on which you must consider carefully whether to play first on your longest suit:

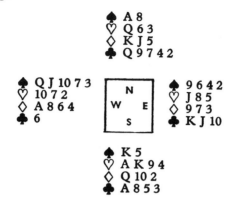

♠ A 8
♡ Q 6 3
◇ K J 5
♣ Q 9 7 4 2

♠ Q J 10 7 3
♡ 10 7 2
◇ A 8 6 4
♣ 6

♠ 9 6 4 2
♡ J 8 5
◇ 9 7 3
♣ K J 10

♠ K 5
♡ A K 9 4
◇ Q 10 2
♣ A 8 5 3

Trick 1

West leads the Queen of spades against 3NT. As South has more entry cards in his own hand than in dummy, he plays low from the table, intending to win with the King. East, following a universal *convention*, drops the 6, a higher card than necessary, to show encouragement for the suit led.

The spade lead has found a weakness. South realises that he can afford to lose the lead only once. The danger of playing on clubs is that if the suit breaks badly, the defence will make two tricks in clubs and at least three in spades before the declarer can run nine tricks.

Looking for other possibilities, South sees that he can easily establish two tricks in diamonds by forcing out the Ace. However, that will be only eight tricks on top. But suppose he can develop a fourth trick in hearts? Then he can turn to diamonds and make his contract without risking the clubs. On this occasion, therefore, the first suit to be tested is the one where only one extra winner can be established.

Tricks 2 to 4

Queen, King, and Ace of hearts. Everyone follows suit to three rounds.

Had the hearts not broken, South would have played Ace and another club. As it is, he can see his way to nine sure tricks.

Trick 5
The thirteenth heart, on which West discards a diamond, dummy a club, and East a diamond.

Trick 6
South leads the 10 of diamonds. West will probably win and clear the spades.

South makes Ace of spades, two tricks in diamonds, and lays down the Ace of clubs. He has made game now, with two spades, four hearts, two diamonds and one club.

When the long suit is needed

Sometimes you will see that the only chance is to play for a favourable division in your long suit.

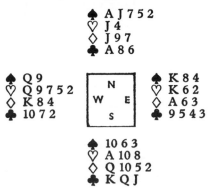

South plays in a borderline contract of 3NT and West leads the 5 of hearts – fourth best from his longest suit.

Trick 1
South plays low from dummy, ensuring two tricks in hearts, however the suit is divided. East plays the King and South wins with the Ace.

Although the diamonds are more solid than the spades, it would be foolish to play on the diamonds here for two reasons. One is that establishing two diamond tricks will give you only eight winners – one in spades, two in hearts, two in diamonds, and three in clubs. The second reason is that the defenders threaten to make two diamonds and three hearts before South can run the tricks he has established.

South has no alternative, therefore, to seeking the extra tricks in spades. Four spades, two hearts, and three clubs will be enough for game.

Trick 2
South leads a low spade, West plays the 9, North the Jack and East the King. There is more than one way of playing the spades, but this is the best. South will develop four tricks if West began with K x or Q x or K Q x or K Q alone.

Trick 3
East returns his partner's suit, leading the 6 of hearts. South plays low and so does West, because he knows that declarer holds the 10 and will make a trick in any event.

Trick 4
In dummy with the Jack of hearts, South lays down the Ace of spades. When the Queen falls, the contract is safe. Declarer leads a spade to the 10 and crosses to the Ace of clubs. He makes four tricks in spades, two in hearts and three in clubs.

Now look at this deal again and consider how South would play, not in 3NT, but in 2NT. Again, a heart lead is covered by the King and Ace. There is a much better case now for playing on diamonds. South can afford to lose two diamonds and three hearts, so the contract will be safe so long as the hearts are breaking not worse than 5–3. On balance, it is certainly better to play on diamonds than on spades. As you see, it is very necessary in this game to keep your eye on the contract.

4

Opening 1NT and Responses

Now that you have an idea of what it is like to play in a notrump contract, it is natural to turn to the general subject of notrump bidding. Of course, you may end up in a notrump contract after a suit opening, but first we will consider hands where the opening bid is 1NT.

In some ways notrump bidding is one of the easiest departments of the game. This is because it can be learned in relation to the dreaded *point count*. You have heard of Bridge players saying, 'I had 13 points, so . . .?' Let me say first that you cannot play Bridge by numbers. On the other hand, reference to the point count does protect an inexperienced player from bad miscalculation. After this left-handed approach, let us consider the animal itself.

The point count

Almost all bridge players use this system of valuation:

$$
\begin{array}{ll}
\text{Ace} & = 4 \text{ points} \\
\text{King} & = 3 \text{ points} \\
\text{Queen} & = 2 \text{ points} \\
\text{Jack} & = 1 \text{ point}
\end{array}
$$

You will appreciate that it is easier to say that a hand contains 13 points than to say that it contains one Ace, two Kings, one Queen, and one Jack. That is the proper way to regard the point count – as a convenient way of summarising high-card values. Make it your servant, not your master.

When to open 1NT

There are, unfortunately, differing standards for an opening 1NT. There is the *weak notrump*, normally 12–14, and the *strong notrump*, either 15–17 or 16–18. Some players announce 'strong notrump', as though proclaiming an undoubted virtue. Others, more attuned to the tournament world, say 'I play a weak notrump throughout'. In this context 'throughout' means vulnerable or not vulnerable. As mentioned briefly in the first chapter, a side that has won a game is vulnerable, which means that the penalties for failing to make a contract are higher.

To play the strong notrump throughout is safe and simple, but the modern tendency is in the direction of the weak notrump. A sensible method, when learning, is to play a 12–14 notrump when not vulnerable, 15–17 when vulnerable.

Provided that the hand falls into the appropriate range, you can open 1NT on most hands that do not contain a *singleton*. The commonest distributions are 4–3–3–3, 4–4–3–2 and 5–3–3–2. These are typical hands on which you would open 1NT when not vulnerable:

♠ K 9 5 2	♠ A 10 4	♠ 10 5
♡ Q 8	♡ Q 5	♡ A Q 8 3
♢ A 10 8 4	♢ K J 9 6 3	♢ K J 9 5
♣ K J 4	♣ Q 8 6	♣ A 9 2
13 points	12 points	14 points

On the following hands you would open with a strong notrump:

♠ A J 9 4	♠ J 4	♠ A 9 6
♡ K 9 3	♡ K Q 10 7 3	♡ K 6 4 2
♢ Q 10 9 4	♢ A J 8	♢ K Q 5
♣ A J	♣ K Q 4	♣ A J 8
15 points	16 points	17 points

The first hand, the one with 15 points, has a good array of 9s and 10s, which can be very useful in the play at notrumps. The second hand contains a five-card major, but that does not disqualify it for 1NT when there are good all-round values.

The following hands, although falling into the range for a strong notrump, are for one reason or another not suited to this bid:

♠ A K 6 5	♠ A 3	♠ A Q J 6 3
♡ A 5 2	♡ K 9 6 4	♡ 5 2
◇ 4 3	◇ A Q 8 6 2	◇ A K J
♣ K Q 7 2	♣ Q 2	♣ J 7 3
16 points	15 points	16 points

The first hand contains a low doubleton and lacks *intermediates* (9s and 10s). An opening One Club is preferable. The second hand has 5–4–2–2 distribution, not ideal for 1NT; open One Diamond. The third hand, weak in two suits, looks more like One Spade than 1NT.

Raises of 1NT

If your partner opens 1NT and your own hand is comparatively balanced, you will normally pass or raise in notrumps. The decision is based on the general proposition that when the combined hands total 25 points there should be a play for game. Therefore, when you can judge immediately that there must be a *minimum* of 25, you will normally raise to 3NT. When you judge that the hands contain a *maximum* of 24, you will generally pass. Remember that there is very small advantage in scoring 70 below for 2NT, rather than 40 below and 30 above. You should never deliberately jeopardise the part score of 40 unless you see chances of game.

Let us see how this general guide works out in practice. Partner opens 1NT not vulnerable and you hold a balanced 10 points. Now the maximum for the two hands is 24 points and you should pass. With 11 points, unless they are particularly barren, you can raise to 2NT. With 12 points you will generally raise to 2NT, sometimes to 3NT.

Special considerations arise when you hold a long minor suit. It is a long way to game in the minor and you should generally aim for 3NT. Partner opens 1NT, not vulnerable, and you hold:

$$\begin{array}{l} ♠ \text{ K 5} \\ ♡ \text{ 7 4 2} \\ ◇ \text{ A Q 10 6 4 3} \\ ♣ \text{ J 5} \end{array}$$

Only 10 points, but you should take a chance on 3NT.
When partner has opened a strong notrump of 15–17, you can

raise to 2NT on 8–9 points, to 3NT on 10 points. Again, give weight to long suits. Partner opens a strong notrump and you hold:

> ♠ K Q 7 4 2
> ♡ Q J 4
> ♢ J 8
> ♣ 10 9 5

Raise to 3NT, counting an extra point for the five-card suit. You should not attempt to play this hand in spades, because it will surely be easier to make nine tricks in notrumps than ten in spades.

To sum up, this is the general advice for raising 1NT:

1 Over a 12–14 notrump, raise to 2NT on 11–12, to 3NT with 13 or a 'good' 12.
2 Over a 15–17 notrump, raise to 2NT on 8–9, to 3NT with 10 or a 'good' 9.

Suit responses to 1NT

A simple take-out of 1NT into Two of a suit is *not* encouraging. Partner opens 1NT, not vulnerable, and you hold:

> (1) ♠ J 9 7 6 3   (2) ♠ A Q 6 5 4
>   ♡ 5   ♡ K 7 3
>   ♢ Q 8 6 4   ♢ Q 8
>   ♣ 9 6 3   ♣ 9 5 2

On (1) take out into Two Spades. You don't expect to make this contract, but you will fare better in spades than your partner in 1NT. Also, you are likely to buy the contract, because the opponents will not find it easy, especially if their strength is divided, to compete at the Three level.

It follows that on (2) you must not make the same bid of Two Spades. You have enough for a raise to 3NT.

A jump to Three of a suit is *forcing*. Partner opens a strong notrump and you hold:

> (3) ♠ A 6 4   (4) ♠ 10 8 7 6 4 2
>   ♡ K 10 8 6 2   ♡ 5
>   ♢ J 9 5 4   ♢ A 10 8 2
>   ♣ 4   ♣ K 3

The 5–4–3–1 distribution of hand (3) is good for suit play and you would jump to Three Hearts. If partner has fair support for hearts he will raise to Four. If he bids 3NT you should let him play there. It is quite likely that he will have both length and strength in your short suit, clubs.

On hand (4) no contract other than Four Spades can be considered, and you could make this bid at once.

When you move into the wide world, you will find that some partners will expect you to play what is known as the *Stayman convention*. When you play this convention, Two Clubs in response to 1NT, whether weak or strong, is a conventional bid, unrelated to clubs, asking the opener to bid Two Hearts or Two Spades with a 4-card suit, and to bid Two Diamonds if he has no 4-card major. Simple as it sounds, this convention has many ramifications. A whole book could be written about it – indeed, more than one has been! To a partner suggesting Stayman, a beginner would be wise to reply: 'If you bid Two Clubs over my 1NT I will make the appropriate rebid, but I don't use the convention myself.'

Rebids by the 1NT opener

Don't tell the same story twice – that is the standing order for a player who has opened 1NT. The opening bid gives a fairly exact picture of the type and range, and, in general, partner should be allowed to determine the final contract.

Over a raise to 2NT bid game unless you are minimum.

Over a suit response at the Two level, *pass*. At most, you may raise to Three with a particularly good fit, when this is necessary to contest against opponents who have overcalled. Never rebid voluntarily 2NT – still less, 3NT.

Over a jump to the Three level, usually raise to Four when you hold three trumps. With only a doubleton in partner's suit, rebid 3NT.

Test of notrump bidding

What is the point count of the following hands? Are they suitable for an opening 1NT not vulnerable?

```
1 ♠ J 9 7 4      2 ♠ K 10 6       3 ♠ Q 4
  ♡ Q 10 8         ♡ A Q J 7 3      ♡ J 9 2
  ◇ K 8 3          ◇ 5 2            ◇ K Q 10 7 4
  ♣ K J 4          ♣ A 6 3          ♣ A J 5
```

Answers
1 10; no, too weak.
2 14; no, 1H is better.
3 13; yes.

What is the point count of the following hands? Are they suitable for an opening 1NT when vulnerable?

```
1 ♠ A 10         2 ♠ K J 7 4      3 ♠ A Q 6 4
  ♡ A Q 7 5 3      ♡ A              ♡ K 8
  ◇ K J 4          ◇ K 10 9 3       ◇ K 9 7 5 3
  ♣ Q 10 8         ♣ A J 7 2        ♣ A J
```

Answers
1 16; yes.
2 16; no, not with a singleton.
3 17; no, 1D is better with 5–4–2–2 distribution.

Partner has opened 1NT not vulnerable. What is your response on the following hands?

```
1 ♠ 9 5 3        2 ♠ 5 3          3 ♠ 7 4
  ♡ K 8 6          ♡ 10 8 4         ♡ K 3
  ◇ A 8 6 4        ◇ K 9 7 5 2      ◇ 8 5 2
  ♣ Q J 9          ♣ A 8 4          ♣ A Q 10 8 5 2
```

Answers
1 Pass; a flat 10 is not enough for a raise.
2 Pass; you are as likely to make 1NT as Two Diamonds.
3 3NT; if partner can bring in the club suit, he will probably make nine tricks.

Partner has opened 1NT, vulnerable. What is your response on the following hands?

1 ♠ Q 10 8 6 3   2 ♠ K 7 3   3 ♠ J
   ♡ 4   ♡ J 8   ♡ 9 7 5 2
   ◇ A 7 5 2   ◇ Q 10 7 5 2   ◇ J 9 8 5 4
   ♣ K 6 3   ♣ Q 6 2   ♣ A 4 3

Answers

1 Three Spades; remember that Two Spades would be a weakness response.

2 2NT; the best hope for game is in notrumps.

3 Two Diamonds; this is likely to be safer than playing in notrumps, though you might make 1NT. Note that, if playing the Stayman convention, it would be unsound to respond Two Clubs, because a rebid of Two Spades by the opener would be inconvenient.

5

The Play in a Suit Contract

Before we look at opening suit bids of One, raises and responses, I think it would be helpful to observe some aspects of the play in suit contracts. The presence of a trump suit brings many new elements into the play. Always the first question is, 'Shall I draw trumps?' We look first at some hands where the declarer has good reason to postpone trump leads.

Taking ruffs in dummy

When the dummy contains a short suit, extra tricks can usually be developed by ruffing this suit. For this reason it may be necessary to postpone trump leads until the losers in declarer's hand have been ruffed.

```
                    ♠ 6
                    ♡ K 7 4
                    ◇ J 8 5 3 2
                    ♣ A 6 5 3
♠ Q 10 8 5 2    ┌─────────┐    ♠ K J 9 3
♡ J 8 2         │    N    │    ♡ 10
◇ Q 9 6 4       │ W     E │    ◇ K 10 7
♣ 10            │    S    │    ♣ Q J 9 8 4
                └─────────┘
                    ♠ A 7 4
                    ♡ A Q 9 6 5 3
                    ◇ A
                    ♣ K 7 2
```

On this occasion you find yourself in Six Hearts, a slam contract. Slams are naturally important, since they carry a bonus that makes them worth twice as much as a game contract, but as a rule they are no more difficult to play than a contract at a much lower level.

With no very attractive lead, West begins with his singleton club. If by chance he could find his partner with the Ace, he might obtain an immediate ruff.

South can count on the top six hearts (unless they break 4–0, which is only a ten per cent chance), two clubs and two Aces. The natural way to develop the extra tricks is to ruff two spades in dummy. The play goes:

Trick 1
Retaining entries to his own hand, South wins the club lead with dummy's Ace.

Trick 2
South leads a spade to the Ace.

Trick 3
He leads a low spade and ruffs with H 4.

Trick 4
He cashes the King of hearts and all follow.

Trick 5
He crosses to the Ace of diamonds.

Trick 6
He leads his last spade and ruffs with dummy's last trump.

The only question now is how to return to hand to draw the remaining trumps. The choice is between ruffing a diamond and leading a club to the King. West, who led a club, is far more likely to hold a singleton club than a singleton diamond, so at Trick 7 declarer leads a diamond and ruffs with a low trump. Then the remaining trumps are drawn and the only loser is the third round of clubs.

On some hands the declarer does not make a frontal attack on the trump suit at any time. Instead, he takes as many ruffs as he can in each hand, aiming to make his trumps separately. This is called *crossruffing*.

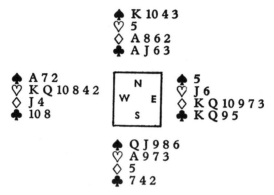

♠ K 10 4 3
♡ 5
♢ A 8 6 2
♣ A J 6 3

♠ A 7 2
♡ K Q 10 8 4 2
♢ J 4
♣ 10 8

♠ 5
♡ J 6
♢ K Q 10 9 7 3
♣ K Q 9 5

♠ Q J 9 8 6
♡ A 9 7 3
♢ 5
♣ 7 4 2

South plays in Four Spades. West's best attack, as the cards lie, is Ace and another trump, but players don't always find the best leads and it is quite likely that West will begin with the King of hearts.

Declarer can count four trump tricks, after the Ace has gone, plus three Aces. The only way to find the extra tricks is by ruffing hearts on the table. Fortunately, he can return easily to his own hand by ruffing diamonds.

Trick 1
South wins with the Ace of hearts.

Trick 2
It is not important on this hand whether declarer begins by ruffing diamonds or hearts. We will say that he first leads a diamond to the Ace.

Trick 3
He ruffs a diamond with the 6 of spades. He must not nervously ruff with a high trump at this stage.

Trick 4

South ruffs a heart with the 3 of spades. Again, he must not panic and ruff high. He needs to ruff three hearts and the time to risk a low trump is on the second round.

Trick 5

South cashes the Ace of clubs. This play is not absolutely essential at the moment, but it is good technique, when crossruffing, to make sure of top winners in the side suits.

The position is now:

```
                 ♠ K 10 4
                 ♡ —
                 ◇ 8 6
                 ♣ J 6 3
    ♠ A 7 2                   ♠ 5
    ♡ Q 10 8 4      N         ♡ —
    ◇ —          W     E      ◇ K 10 9 7
    ♣ 8             S         ♣ K Q 9
                 ♠ Q J 9 8
                 ♡ 9 7
                 ◇ —
                 ♣ 7 4
```

The lead is in dummy and South leads a diamond, ruffing with S 8. West may overruff and return a trump, but this will not help the defence. It would be better play for West to discard. Now South declarer can afford to ruff the next heart with a high trump. He continues the high crossruff, losing eventually two clubs and one trump.

There were a number of possible traps in the play. First, it would have been a mistake to lead even one round of trumps. This would have given the defence a chance, either now or later, to play a second round, preventing South from ruffing three hearts in dummy. Second, it was essential to ruff the first diamond (also the first heart) with a low trump. Suppose that South had ruffed the first diamond with S 8, the next with S 9, and so on; eventually West would have held the A 7 2 of spades over South's Q 6. Finally, South had to cash the Ace of clubs before West was able to discard two clubs on diamond leads.

Establishing a suit by ruffing

One of the most important functions of the trump suit is to enable the declarer to establish a broken suit without losing tricks in the process. In this example South establishes his own side suit by ruffing in dummy.

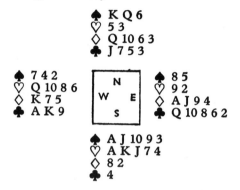

♠ K Q 6
♡ 5 3
◇ Q 10 6 3
♣ J 7 5 3

♠ 7 4 2
♡ Q 10 8 6
◇ K 7 5
♣ A K 9

♠ 8 5
♡ 9 2
◇ A J 9 4
♣ Q 10 8 6 2

♠ A J 10 9 3
♡ A K J 7 4
◇ 8 2
♣ 4

South plays in Four Spades. If South had shown his heart suit during the bidding, West might have led a trump, to prevent the ruffs, but we will suppose instead that he begins with the King of clubs. (The King is the traditional lead from a suit headed by A K, though many players nowadays prefer to lead the Ace from A K, the King from K Q.) As usual, we will follow the early play trick by trick.

Trick 1
West leads the King of clubs. East, holding strong clubs, may signal encouragement by dropping the 8.

Trick 2
Seeing the dummy, West may *switch* to a trump. We will consider this possibility later. Alternatively, West may follow with the Ace of clubs, which South will ruff.

Tricks 3 and 4
With two diamonds and a club to lose, declarer must aim to establish his heart suit without losing a trick. Instead of risking the finesse, he plays off Ace and King of hearts, to which all follow.

Trick 5

South ruffs a heart with the Queen of spades. It would be foolish to ruff with the 6, risking an overruff.

Trick 6

When East *shows out*, discarding a club, South realises that he will need to ruff again to establish his last heart. He returns to hand by leading the 6 of spades to the 9.

Trick 7

South leads a fourth round of hearts, ruffing with dummy's last trump, the King.

Trick 8

Declarer comes back to hand by ruffing a club.

At this stage South must hope that the three trumps still against him will be divided 2–1. (Having ruffed twice himself, he has only two trumps left.) The trumps fall, and declarer makes his tenth trick with the fifth heart.

Do you think it would have made any difference if West had led a trump at Trick 2? South would win in his own hand, since he proposes to use dummy's high trumps for ruffing. As before, he cashes the top hearts and ruffs a heart with S Q. He returns to hand with a club ruff, trumps the next heart with S K, and is still in control. He can ruff another club, draw trumps, and make the last heart.

The club lead was doubly unfortunate for the defence, because it established *communication* between declarer and dummy. Despite the trump switch at Trick 2 South was able to ruff hearts twice without losing the lead. An opening trump lead, or a diamond followed by a trump, would defeat the contract, because South would not be able to go from hand to hand without letting the defenders gain the lead to play a second round of trumps.

On this next deal declarer uses his own trumps to establish a long suit in dummy:

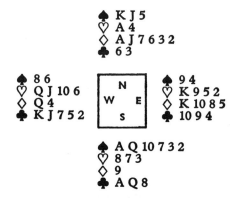

The contract is Six Spades and West leads the Queen of hearts. There are two possible lines. South could take the club finesse and aim to ruff the third round of clubs and also the third round of hearts. This way, assuming the club King to be on the right side for him, he would lose just one heart trick. Alternatively, South can attempt to set up dummy's diamonds. It is not practicable to combine the two possibilities, because if South is going to play on diamonds he will need all the entries to dummy. The diamonds in fact offer the better chance, so the play goes:

Trick 1
South wins with the Ace of hearts in dummy.

Trick 2
Ace of diamonds. It is essential to begin ruffing diamonds at once, conserving the trump entries to dummy.

Trick 3
A low diamond from dummy. East would not be so foolish as to play the King, because it is obvious from the play that South has the singleton, not Q x. South ruffs.

Trick 4
A spade to the Jack.

Trick 5
A diamond ruffed with the Queen. West shows out.

Trick 6
A spade to the Jack. South is pleased to see that both opponents follow.

The position is now:

```
              ♠ 5
              ♡ 4
              ◇ J 7 6
              ♣ 6 3

♠ —                        ♠ —
♡ J 10 6      N            ♡ K 9 2
◇ —         W   E          ◇ K
♣ K J 7 5     S            ♣ 10 9 4

              ♠ A 3
              ♡ 8 7
              ◇ —
              ♣ A Q 8
```

The lead is in dummy. South ruffs the last diamond and leads a heart. If East wins and leads a club, South goes up with the Ace, ruffs a heart, and discards two clubs on the long diamonds.

Playing on the diamond suit, the declarer needed to find either diamonds 3–3 or diamonds 4–2 and spades 2–2. An experienced player, having seen such a hand many times, would see this quickly and would know that to bring in the diamonds represented a better chance than the finesse in clubs.

A ruffing finesse

Another valuable play in a suit contract is the 'ruffing finesse'. The declarer is often able to play either opponent for a critical card. In this example the ruffing finesse is safer than a straight finesse:

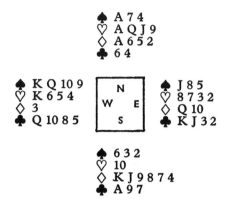

    ♠ A 7 4
    ♡ A Q J 9
    ◇ A 6 5 2
    ♣ 6 4

♠ K Q 10 9   ♠ J 8 5
♡ K 6 5 4   ♡ 8 7 3 2
◇ 3   ◇ Q 10
♣ Q 10 8 5   ♣ K J 3 2

    ♠ 6 3 2
    ♡ 10
    ◇ K J 9 8 7 4
    ♣ A 9 7

    South plays in Five Diamonds and West leads the King of spades. Even if he can pick up the diamonds safely, declarer is still in danger of losing two spades and one club. He could take a simple finesse in hearts, hoping for a discard on the Ace of hearts, but if the finesse were to lose, the defenders would beat the contract immediately with two spades and one heart.

    It is much safer to take a ruffing finesse in hearts. The play goes:

Trick 1
South wins in dummy with the Ace of spades.

Trick 2
He leads the Ace of diamonds from dummy and is careful to *unblock*, dropping the 7 from hand, not the 4. I say 'is careful', but in fact such plays, maintaining a fluent position, should be made automatically. Here you will find that the 4 of diamonds becomes a vital card.

Trick 3
A diamond to the King, West discarding a club.

Trick 4
The 10 of hearts to the Ace.

Declarer has arrived at this position:

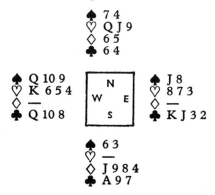

♠ 7 4
♡ Q J 9
◇ 6 5
♣ 6 4

♠ Q 10 9
♡ K 6 5 4
◇ —
♣ Q 10 8

♠ J 8
♡ 8 7 3
◇ —
♣ K J 3 2

♠ 6 3
♡ —
◇ J 9 8 4
♣ A 9 7

He now leads the Queen of hearts from dummy. If East held the King and covered, South would ruff with D 8, enter dummy by leading D 4, and take two discards. As the cards lie, East plays low on the Queen of hearts. South discards a spade and West wins with H K. The defenders play two rounds of spades. South, who had only one spade left, ruffs the second round with D 8, enters dummy with a trump, and discards two clubs on H J 9.

You see that, playing in this fashion, the declarer succeeds whether West or East holds the King of hearts.

6

Opening Suit Bids of One and Responses

Bidding is a partnership enterprise. When you open with a suit bid of One you say in effect: 'I have a better than average hand in high cards. Even if my suit does not fit your hand, you will find that I have some cards that will be useful to you in your own long suit.' If this sort of understanding did not exist, there would be no foundation for constructive bidding.

The range for bids of One
The majority of hands within the 12 to 20 points range, if not suitable for 1NT, are opened with a bid of One in a suit. You notice how I put that? Not as an injunction, 'With 12 to 20 points you must open One of a suit (or 1NT).' That kind of pronouncement ignores too many important considerations.

There is universal agreement that an opening bid of One must contain a sound *rebid*. If your partner responds in a new suit, in a sequence such as One Heart–One Spade, or One Spade–Two Clubs, you must keep the bidding open (unless partner has passed originally), and your rebid, though it may be minimum, must be sound. You must have this in mind whenever you open. The strength of your suit is important, and for this reason there are different standards for opening bids with a six-card suit and shorter suits.

When you hold a six-card suit
A good six-card suit is first-class insurance against a *misfit*.

♠ K Q J 10 7 4
♡ 6 3
♢ A 8 5 2
♣ 4

This is not merely a sound opening in any position and at any score, but a powerful hand. The suit is strong – you could play safely in spades even if partner held a singleton or *void*. By opening One Spade, the highest-ranking suit, you make it more dangerous for opponents to intervene. And the 6–4–2–1 distribution makes your hand more powerful than if you had a more balanced shape, such as 6–3–2–2. Finally, it is an asset that your high cards coincide with your long suits. Compare this hand with another that contains a six-card suit and 10 points:

♠ 5 3
♡ Q 8 6 4 3 2
♢ A 6 4
♣ K J

This is nothing like so good a hand. The most important difference is that now, if your partner has no support for your hearts, the suit is far from self-supporting. Not vulnerable, you might open this hand as a tactical measure in third position, after two passes, but otherwise it would be a poor opening.

In short, with a good six-card suit, especially a major suit, you can often open with 10 or 11 points.

When you hold a five-card suit
The most promising hands are those that contain values in both majors, such as:

♠ K Q 10 8 4
♡ A Q 10 6
♢ 3
♣ 9 6 2

It is safe to open One Spade in all circumstances, because you have a sound rebid of Two Hearts.

Any hand with two five-card suits is potentially good:

Again, you can open with 11 points, because if the hearts do not fit your partner, the diamonds may. The fact that the suits are adjacent makes it easier to develop your hand. Open the higher-ranking suit, hearts, even though the diamonds are stronger.

This type of hand may prove awkward:

♠ J 7
♡ K 8 6 4 2
◇ 4
♣ A Q 7 4 3

It is dangerous to open One Heart, because you have no good rebid over a *response* of Two Diamonds. It would be unthinkable to advance to the Three level, so you would have to rebid the poor hearts. (Remember that you must never pass a suit-over-suit response, unless your partner has passed originally.) You might, it is true, open with One Club, but it is not normal to suppress a five-card major, and again you might have problems on the next round. This hand, therefore, is not a sound opening.

In playing strength and general flexibility there is a considerable difference between these two hands, which both contain the same honour cards, differently placed:

The first hand is quite easy to manage. You open One Diamond, bidding the longer suit first, and if partner responds in your weak suit, hearts, you have a convenient rebid of One Spade. The most awkward responses for your hand are 1NT and 2NT. You could rebid Two Diamonds over 1NT, but 2NT you must pass.

The objection to opening One Club on the second hand is that you are not well placed over responses of either One Spade or

1NT. This would certainly be an unwise opening if you were vulnerable.

When you hold only four-card suits

When you hold only four-card suits and cannot consider 1NT because the hand does not fall within the appropriate range (12–14 not vulnerable, 15–17 vulnerable), the general rule is to bid the suit below your own shortest suit. The borderline is 12 points, because it is normal to open any hand with 13, and if you have only 11 and no long suit it can hardly be wrong to pass. We will look first at some borderline hands:

$$(3) \spadesuit \text{A K 10 4} \qquad (4) \spadesuit \text{A Q 8 4}$$
$$\heartsuit \text{7 4} \qquad \qquad \heartsuit \text{J 4}$$
$$\diamondsuit \text{9 6 3} \qquad \qquad \diamondsuit \text{K Q 6 3}$$
$$\clubsuit \text{A J 9 6} \qquad \qquad \clubsuit \text{6 3 2}$$

It is safe enough to open hand (3). You open One Club, not One Spade, and have a simple rebid over a response in either red suit. Hand (4) is a type on which it is advisable to pass. If you open One Spade you have no good rebid over a response of Two Hearts, and if you open One Diamond you have nothing good to say over a response of Two Clubs. Some players would open 1NT, but this is most unattractive on a minimum with all the strength in two suits.

On the next two hands the problem is which suit to bid first:

$$(5) \spadesuit \text{A Q 8 6} \qquad (6) \spadesuit \text{K Q 10 7}$$
$$\heartsuit \text{A 7 4} \qquad \qquad \heartsuit \text{4}$$
$$\diamondsuit \text{K J 9 5} \qquad \qquad \diamondsuit \text{A J 9 7}$$
$$\clubsuit \text{6 2} \qquad \qquad \clubsuit \text{K 8 6 3}$$

On hand (5) open One Spade, the suit 'below' your doubleton. Over Two Hearts you can raise to Three Hearts, and over Two Clubs you can rebid in diamonds or (if your bidding system permits) notrumps. On hand (6) open One Diamond, the suit below the singleton.

Finally, there are occasions when the only sound opening is in a three-card minor. Suppose that you hold:

$$(7) \spadesuit \text{A 9 4} \qquad (8) \spadesuit \text{A 8 6 4}$$
$$\heartsuit \text{K 8 7 4} \qquad \qquad \heartsuit \text{A K J}$$
$$\diamondsuit \text{A 10 5} \qquad \qquad \diamondsuit \text{A K 5}$$
$$\clubsuit \text{Q 6 3} \qquad \qquad \clubsuit \text{6 4 2}$$

On hand (7) you can open 1NT if not vulnerable. If vulnerable, or if playing a strong notrump throughout, you must open One Club. It is undesirable to open a weak major suit on a minimum hand. On (8) the best opening, vulnerable or not, is One Diamond.

The first response to an opening bid

Responses to an opening bid of One fall into six main groups:

- (*a*) Pass – the weakest call, evidently.
- (*b*) Responses that immediately limit the strength. There are two such responses – 1NT and a single raise, from One to Two.
- (*c*) Bids of variable strength – a simple response in a new suit, such as One Heart over One Diamond, or Two Clubs over One Spade.
- (*d*) Bids that are encouraging but not forcing. The principle examples are 2NT and a *double raise*, from One to Three.
- (*e*) Game bids, such as 3NT or a raise to game.
- (*f*) Jump bids in a new suit, forcing to game. Three Clubs over One Spade is a *force*, and so is Two Hearts over One Diamond.

We look at these responses in turn.

(*a*) *When to pass*

It is advisable to pass on most hands of less than 6 points unless they contain either a good suit or distributional support for partner's suit. Also pass on a barren 6-point hand that does not present a simple bid at the range of One.

On hand (1) pass One Spade, respond One Heart to One Diamond or One Club. On (2) it would not be a mistake to pass any opening bid, but many players would respond 1NT to One

Spade, One Heart to One Diamond or One Club. In other words, it is a borderline hand.

Do not be tempted, when you hold a weak hand with a long suit, to seek to improve what seems to be a poor contract.

```
(3) ♠ 5
    ♡ 8 7 4 2
    ◇ Q J 9 7 4 2
    ♣ 6 3
```

Pass One Spade. Probably Two Diamonds would be a better contract, but the bidding won't stop there. Meanwhile, you mislead partner concerning your general strength.

(b) Comparatively weak responses – 1NT and a simple raise
There are two responses that limit your hand at once. These are 1NT and a single raise. 1NT is a very frequent response on moderate balanced hands in the range of 6 to 9. It is usually right to prefer a response in a four-card major at the One level, but don't make a rule of this.

```
(4) ♠ J 7 3        (5) ♠ 7 2
    ♡ K 10 5           ♡ Q 10 8 4
    ◇ Q J 5            ◇ A 8 3
    ♣ Q 6 4 2          ♣ J 5 4 2
```

On hand (4) respond 1NT to any opening bid of One, including One Club. The range for 1NT over One Club is more like 7 to 10 than 6 to 9; with weaker hands respond, if at all, in the lowest four-card suit. On (5) respond 1NT to One Spade, One Heart to One Diamond or One Club. You have the values for a raise of One Club to Two Clubs, but a response of One Heart is more constructive.

The other limited response is the single raise from One to Two. When you hold fair support for partner's major suit, raise his suit in preference to any other call. Points are not important in this area of bidding, though it is true to say that any hand with more than 10 points would be too strong for a simple raise. Do you recall hand (3) above?

```
♠ 5
♡ 8 7 4 2
◇ Q J 9 7 4 2
♣ 6 3
```

It is perfectly in order, with four trumps and a singleton, to raise One Heart to Two Hearts. If the hand were still weaker, with 2–4–5–2 distribution instead of 1–4–6–2, it would still be tactically correct to raise. Some players are taught to use a so-called 'distributional count' that allots points to short suits and trump support as well as to high cards. I have doubts about this for two reasons. The first is that raises have a tactical purpose, which an assessment by points does not take into account. The second is that a player who ties himself to such artificial reckoning will never acquire a good idea of valuation. It is better to make mistakes on the way than to petrify your judgment.

These are by way of being maximum raises from One Spade to Two Spades:

(6) ♠ K 10 7 4   (7) ♠ Q 9 8
    ♡ 5 2   ♡ K 7 5 3
    ◇ A 9 6 4 3   ◇ K 7 6 4 2
    ♣ J 2   ♣ 3

The second hand contains only three trumps, but Two Spades is preferable to Two Diamonds. (Over One Heart you would raise to Three Hearts.)

One warning: don't be over-impressed by long and strong trump support. Partner opens One Heart and you hold:

(8) ♠ Q 4 2
    ♡ A Q J 5 2
    ◇ 6 5 3
    ♣ 7 4

The hand contains many losers and is worth only a raise to Two Hearts.

A single raise in a minor suit is made only on hands that offer no more constructive response.

(9) ♠ J 7 4   (10) ♠ Q 8 6 4
    ♡ K 3   ♡ 7 4
    ◇ K 8 5 3   ◇ Q 2
    ♣ 10 7 4 2   ♣ 10 8 7 4 3

On (9) raise One Diamond to Two Diamonds. Over One Club prefer One Diamond to a raise. On (10) raise One Club to Two Clubs. It would be unsound to respond One Spade and follow with support for clubs.

(c) Bids of variable strength – a new suit at minimum level

A simple response at the One level has a wide range, as may be seen from these two examples:

(11) ♠ K J 10 6 4 2   (12) ♠ A J 8 4 3
     ♡ 5   ♡ K Q 4
     ♢ 10 7 3   ♢ A Q 7 6
     ♣ 8 4 2   ♣ 5

On (11) respond One Spade to any opening bid of One. You are under strength in high cards, but nothing very bad can happen. You may even find a good fit. In any case, it is better tactics to bid than to give opponents a free run.

On (12) it would not be a mistake to bid Two Spades over One Club, but the modern style is to keep the bidding low when there are several features to show and you cannot be sure where you will end up. You would jump in response to One Heart or One Diamond, but not necessarily over One Club.

With suits of unequal length it is usually correct to bid the longer suit first. An exception occurs when you are too weak for a response at the Two level.

(13) ♠ K 10 7 4
     ♡ 5 2
     ♢ Q J 8 6 3
     ♣ 6 3

Here you would respond One Diamond to One Club, but over One Heart you must bid One Spade, not Two Diamonds.

When you hold two four-card suits it is usual to bid 'upwards'. Partner opens One Diamond and you hold:

(14) ♠ K J 9 3
     ♡ A 10 8 3
     ♢ Q 4
     ♣ J 7 3

Over One Club or One Diamond, respond One Heart. This gives the *opener* an easy chance to show a second suit of spades.

The requirements for a new suit at the Two level are higher. You need either about 10 points or a long, rebiddable suit.

(15) ♠ 6 3   (16) ♠ 6 5 2
     ♡ Q 4   ♡ 4
     ♢ A J 8 6 3   ♢ J 7 3
     ♣ Q 7 3 2   ♣ A Q J 9 6 3

Hand (15) is a minimum for Two Diamonds over One Spade or One Heart. On (16) you can venture Two Clubs (more happily over One Spade than over One Heart) because the suit is rebiddable.

On stronger hands there is no objection to a response in a minor suit at the Two level on a four-card suit. Partner opens One Spade and you hold:

(17) ♠ J 4
     ♡ A Q 7 5
     ◇ 6 4 3
     ♣ A Q 8 2

Respond Two Clubs. A response of Two Hearts normally implies a five-card suit.

(d) Encouraging bids – 2NT and a double raise

The range for 2NT is from 11 points to a flat 13. The bid should be avoided with a singleton in partner's suit or a low doubleton in any side suit. Partner opens One Spade and you hold:

(18) ♠ 5   (19) ♠ K 10 5
     ♡ K 10 8 3   ♡ A J 8 4
     ◇ A Q 7 4   ◇ Q 10 8
     ♣ Q J 5 2   ♣ Q 9 2

It is a mistake, on hand (18), to think: 'Partner has bid spades and I have the other suits well wrapped up, so I will bid 2NT.' Partner is entitled to think you have some support for spades and may jump to Four Spades. You can *approach* here with Two Clubs or Two Diamonds. If 3NT is the best contract, you should get there eventually. On hand (19) you can respond 2NT to One Spade. In response to One Club or One Diamond some players would bid a scientific One Heart, but my choice would be 2NT.

For a double raise of partner's major suit you need, roughly speaking, about 9 to 11 points with four trumps and a doubleton, or about 7 to 9 points with four trumps and a singleton. Partner opens One Heart and you hold:

(20) ♠ K 4   (21) ♠ 10 8 4
     ♡ J 10 8 5   ♡ K 10 8 3
     ◇ A Q 3   ◇ A 7 6 4 2
     ♣ 7 6 4 2   ♣ 3

Both hands are sound raises to Three Hearts. Note that on (21) you do not consider a response of Two Diamonds. The only effect of this would be to make it easier for the opponents to intervene.

A double raise of partner's minor suit is likely to be based on distribution and trump support. Partner opens One Diamond and you hold:

(22)	♠ 8 5	(23)	♠ A 7 5
	♡ Q 3		♡ 4
	◊ A Q 8 6 4		◊ K Q 10 8
	♣ Q 7 4 3		♣ J 7 5 3 2

In each case you raise to Three Diamonds because no other bid looks remotely sensible.

(e) Game bids – 3NT or a raise to game

A response of 3NT suggests about 13 to 15 points. Though a favourite with many players, this is not, in general, a good bid to choose unless your distribution is a balanced 4–3–3–3. This is because it is difficult, after 3NT, to find a delicate fit in a suit divided 4–4. Partner opens One Heart and you hold:

(24)	♠ A K 4	(25)	♠ K 10 7
	♡ Q 2		♡ J 7 5
	◊ K 10 8 4		◊ A Q 8 3
	♣ K 7 5 3		♣ K J 3

On (24) prefer to approach with Two Clubs. Hand (25) is the right type for 3NT.

A raise to game in a major has two faces. It may be a hand somewhat stronger than a raise to Three, or it may be to some extent a *shut-out* bid on a hand that is powerful only in distribution.

(26)	♠ K 4	(27)	♠ 5 2
	♡ A 10 8 5		♡ Q J 9 6 2
	◊ A Q 3		◊ —
	♣ 7 6 4 2		♣ 10 7 6 4 3 2

Hand (26) is the same as (20), except that it has the Ace of hearts instead of the Jack. Now you must raise One Heart to Four Hearts. Hand (27) is a very different type, but again you would raise to game in the hope of shutting out the opponents.

If the fit is reasonably good – that is to say, if partner's strength is in the right places – you may well make Four Hearts.

(f) Jump bids in a new suit

With a very strong hand you can jump in a new suit. Such a response is forcing to game. Partner opens One Spade and you hold:

(28)	♠ K J 7 3	(29)	♠ 7 4
	♡ 4		♡ A 10
	◊ A 6 2		◊ A K Q 9 6 3
	♣ A Q 10 7 3		♣ K 6 5

The first hand is too strong for a direct raise to Four Spades. You must 'force' with Three Clubs and bid at least Four Spades on the next round. On the second hand force with Three Diamonds, intending to bid 3NT over a rebid of Three Hearts or Three Spades.

As remarked earlier in connection with hand (12), it is not always necessary to force even when your hand is certainly strong enough for game. Some hands require time for development. For example, partner opens One Diamond and you hold:

(30)	♠ A Q 6 5
	♡ K J 10 3
	◊ Q
	♣ K Q 4 2

The best move is to respond simply One Heart. As we shall see in the next chapter, there are various ways of ensuring that the bidding will not be dropped short of game. To get a picture of partner's hand, you must keep the bidding low at first.

Some special situations

In this section we look briefly at four special situations. They are:

    (a) Responding on a limited hand with a long suit.
    (b) Responding after a pass.
    (c) Responding over intervention.
    (d) Bidding from a part score.

(a) Responding on a long suit

Occasionally you will hold a long suit and will want to convey to partner that your hand is suitable for play in this suit only. Depending on the strength, you may respond with a double jump, or with a jump to game. Partner opens One Diamond and you hold:

(1)   ♠ 5
       ♡ K Q 10 9 8 5 3
       ◊ 7 4
       ♣ Q 4 3

(2)   ♠ A K J 10 8 7 4
       ♡ 6
       ◊ 4
       ♣ J 10 7 3

On (1) it would not be a mistake to respond simply One Heart, but a double jump to Three Hearts is better. It conveys the nature of the holding and makes it more difficult for the opponents to intervene. It is most important, of course, to distinguish between a response of Two Hearts, a strong force, and Three Hearts, a relatively weak bid on a long suit. On (2) it would be sensible to respond Four Spades, showing a powerful hand with limited strength in high cards.

(b) Responding after a pass

When you have passed originally, most responses have the same sense as usual, but responder must bear in mind that simple changes of suit are no longer forcing. It is thus advisable to avoid delicate responses at the Two level when a more constructive response is available. Partner opens One Spade and you hold:

♠ Q J 7
♡ 5 2
◊ A 6 4 3
♣ K 9 5 2

The danger of bidding Two Clubs is that partner may pass. It is better to raise to Three Spades, although you have only three trumps.

A player who has passed will never hold the values for an orthodox forcing response. A jump in a new suit by a passed hand is conventionally understood to mean that you hold strong support for partner's suit. The bidding goes:

South	West	North	East
No	No	1H	No
?			

South holds:

(3) ♠ K J 7 4 2   (4) ♠ 7
    ♡ 5 4   ♡ K J 10 8
    ♢ A 10 7 3   ♢ 6 4 2
    ♣ Q 6   ♣ A Q 9 6 4

On hand (3) bid simply One Spade. Do not bid Two Spades
to show that you had a good pass. On (4) jump to Three Clubs.
The message is that you have strong support for hearts and values
in clubs.

(c) Responding over intervention

The main difference is that you are no longer obliged to give
what used to be called a 'courtesy response' on moderate values.
Say that the bidding goes:

South	West	North	East
—	—	1D	1S
?			

South holds:

(5) ♠ Q 10 6
    ♡ Q 8 5 4
    ♢ 6 4 2
    ♣ K 7 6

South would have responded One Heart if East had passed,
but after the intervention he must pass.

On the other hand, responder should not suppress distributional support. The bidding goes:

South	West	North	East
—	—	1S	2D
?			

South holds:

♠ Q 10 7 4
♡ 5 4
♢ 7 3
♣ Q 9 6 4 2

Although close to minimum for a raise, South should take the opportunity to indicate support with Two Spades.

(d) Bidding from a part score

The general scheme of opening bids is not altered by possession of a part score. There may be a temptation, when you are 40 up, to 'bid to the score' – to open Two Hearts, for example, on a hand that is well short of the normal requirements for a Two bid (see Chapter 7). This is not self-evidently wrong, but it is contrary to normal practice. You may, however, extend the range of 1NT when this would be enough for game.

Similarly, it is better, when responding, to preserve the normal standards and not to make a series of adjustments. When both players stretch because of the part score, the final contract will be impossible. Furthermore, if opening bids and responses are not reasonably sound, the partners will have no basis on which to judge their values when the opponents compete, as they usually will.

Summary of opening bids and responses

We have covered a lot of ground in this chapter and you may like to check that you have the main points in mind.

Opening bids of One

Usually in the range of 12 to 20, may be less with a good six-card suit or two five-card suits. As a rule, bid the longer suit first. With suits of equal length, generally open the higher-ranking with 5–5. With only four-card suits, usually open the suit below the short suit.

The first response

Pass with less than 6 points unless you have a fair suit that can be bid at the level of One.

Respond 1NT on 6 to 9, 2NT on 11 to 13, 3NT on (a good) 13 to 15.

Responses in a new suit at the One level have a wide range, from about 5 to (occasionally) 18.

A raise to Two is comparatively weak, a raise to Three invites game, a raise to Four may be based on values, may be a shut-out.

A response at the Two level suggests a minimum of 9 points but may be made on less when the suit is long and strong.

A jump response in a new suit is forcing to game.

Make sure that you fully understand this chapter before you proceed to the next. It is excellent practice to deal four hands, pick out one on which you would open the bidding, and then consider how you would respond with each of the other three.

Test of Opening Bids

What would you open on the following hands?

1 ♠ K J
  ♡ 7 4 2
  ◇ A Q 6 4 3
  ♣ J 6 3

2 ♠ A K J 5
  ♡ 6 4
  ◇ K J 8 5 2
  ♣ 5 3

3 ♠ 5
  ♡ K Q 5 2
  ◇ A J 8 4
  ♣ K 7 4 2

Answers

1 Pass. You have only 11 points, your main suit is a minor, and the concentration of strength in spades is not a good feature.
2 1D, the longer suit.
3 1H, the suit below the singleton; but 1D would not be a mistake.

Test of responses

Your partner opens One Heart. What would you respond on the following hands?

1 ♠ 6 3 2
  ♡ Q 7 4
  ◇ K 9 6 4 3
  ♣ Q 6

2 ♠ Q 9 6 4
  ♡ 5
  ◇ A 8 3
  ♣ J 8 6 4 2

3 ♠ 7 6
  ♡ 5 4
  ◇ 10 8 3
  ♣ K Q 7 6 4 2

Answers

1 2H. You cannot consider responding at the Two level, and the raise to 2H is likely to be of more interest to partner than a response of 1NT.
2 1S. There is no harm in bidding shaded suits at the One level.

If you respond 1NT partner will tend to assume that you have no length in spades.

3 Pass. This might occasionally lead to a missed game, but 2C would be unsound and 1NT would not give a good picture.

Your partner opens One Club. What would you respond on the following hands?

1 ♠ 5 3
♡ K J 5 3
◇ Q 8 7 2
♣ 10 7 4

2 ♠ J 8 7 5 3
♡ A Q 8 4 2
◇ K 5
♣ 2

3 ♠ 10 5
♡ A Q 2
◇ K 8 4
♣ Q J 8 4 2

Answers

1 1D, bidding 'upwards' on a weak hand with only four-card suits.

2 1S, the higher-ranking of five-card suits.

3 1D. You have the values for a double raise to 3C, but with 12 points you should look for a more constructive approach. For example, if opener can rebid in spades you can jump in no-trumps; if he raises the diamonds you can show your support for clubs.

Your partner opens One Spade. What would you respond on the following hands?

1 ♠ K 7 3
♡ A Q 6 4
◇ K 10 8 3
♣ 5 2

2 ♠ Q
♡ K 7 4
◇ A K 8 5
♣ A J 9 6 3

3 ♠ A 5 3
♡ A J 8 4
◇ 3
♣ 10 8 6 4 2

Answers

1 2D. When responding in a four-card suit, prefer a minor to 2H.

2 2C. You have the values for a forcing response of 3C, but this is a type of hand that may require time for development. You will always be able to keep the bidding alive on the next round.

3 3S. 2C would not be a mistake, but this is one of the rare hands where a double raise on three trumps seems the best answer. The disadvantage of bidding 2C is that if partner had a strong hand with something like K x x in clubs he would imagine that he had a good fit in this suit.

7

The Second Round

If his first bid has been well chosen, the opener's rebid is seldom difficult. The best way to tackle this subject is to consider the opener's action in face of the various types of response described in the last chapter. As we go along, we may comment also on subsequent action by the responder.

Opener's first rebid

We will observe in turn:

- (a) The rebid over 1NT.
- (b) The rebid over a single raise.
- (c) The rebid over a new suit at the One level.
- (d) The rebid over a new suit at the Two level.
- (e) The rebid over 2NT.
- (f) The rebid over a double raise.
- (g) The rebid over a force.

(a) The rebid over 1NT
This is one of the trickiest areas of bidding, because of the temptation to *overbid*. Suppose you have a good-looking hand such as:

♠ Q 7
♡ K J 9 6 3
◇ A 8 4
♣ K Q 4

Not vulnerable, you open One Heart and partner responds 1NT. What is your first reaction? Many players would raise to 2NT, some to 3NT.

Now say that partner has 8 points, which is in the upper range of his expected 6 to 9. You will still have only 23 points in the combined hands, which in most cases will not be enough for game. So you should pass 1NT. As always, you may take long suits into account, but in general you need 17 to 18 to suggest game in notrumps. With 19 you can raise to 3NT.

When you have a singleton or void, you may either repeat your first suit or introduce a second suit. After 1H–1NT you hold:

(1)	♠ 7	(2)	♠ K 10 7
	♡ K J 8 6 4 2		♡ A Q 9 6 4
	◇ K 7 4 2		◇ 5
	♣ A 6		♣ K J 7 2

On (1) take out into Two Hearts. On (2) bid Two Clubs, not Two Hearts. Partner may hold four or five clubs and be short in hearts.

Beware, however, of taking out into a suit that is higher ranking than your first suit. After the same sequence, 1H–1NT, you hold:

(3)	♠ A Q 7 4
	♡ K 9 7 5 2
	◇ 5
	♣ K J 6

There are two reasons why it would be wrong to bid Two Spades. One is that you would be taking the bidding too high on a minimum hand, the other, that partner has had a chance to respond One Spade and has not done so. He cannot, therefore, hold a fair hand including a four-card spade suit. Best is to pass 1NT.

With a stronger hand you may make a jump rebid or bid a suit that is higher than your first. After 1D–1NT you hold:

(4)	♠ A 5 3	(5)	♠ 4
	♡ 6		♡ A K 10 6
	◇ A Q J 9 6 4		◇ K Q J 8 4
	♣ K Q 7		♣ A 9 5

On (4) rebid Three Diamonds, on (5) Two Hearts.

If stronger still, you may jump to game or jump in a new suit. After 1S–1NT you hold:

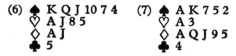

(6) ♠ K Q J 10 7 4   (7) ♠ A K 7 5 2
    ♡ A J 8 5   ♡ A 3
    ◇ A J   ◇ A Q J 9 5
    ♣ 5   ♣ 4

On (6) you would jump to Four Spades and on (7) you would force with Three Diamonds.

Responder's action

A player who has responded 1NT should always pass a minimum rebid of opener's suit. The sequence 1H–1NT–2H–2NT is self-evidently wrong. When opener has changed the suit, as in 1H–1NT–2D, responder may pass 2D, or raise to 3D, or return to 2H, or, occasionally, jump to 3H. He should rarely persist with 2NT.

(b) The rebid over a single raise

This is another situation where players tend to overbid. After 1S–2S you need about 17, or a good 16, to suggest game in no-trumps. As a rough guide, if you could take an Ace away from your hand and still have a sound opening, you may try for game. After 1H–2H you hold:

(1) ♠ K 4   (2) ♠ K 7 6
    ♡ A Q J 8 5   ♡ A K 9 7 4
    ◇ K 9 4 2   ◇ 5
    ♣ 10 3   ♣ A J 8 2

On (1) do not consider any advance over Two Hearts. On (2) you are worth a game try. A new suit, Three Clubs, would be a *trial bid,* forcing for one round. You may take it as a general principle that when a new suit is mentioned after a raise, the new suit is forcing and may not be a genuine suit at all.

Responder's action

When opener makes a game try over a single raise, responder should accept unless minimum. Consider these two hands in partnership:

```
West              East
♠ K Q 10 7 4      ♠ J 9 5 2
♡ A J 5           ♡ 8 6 3
◇ 9 3             ◇ A 8 6 2
♣ A K 5           ♣ Q 6
```

West opens One Spade and East raises to Two Spades. West is not quite strong enough to go to Four Spades, so he makes a trial bid of Three Clubs. East, who has a moderate but not minimum raise, should then jump to game, bidding Four Spades. West has a good chance to make this contract; he will discard a heart from dummy on the third round of clubs and should lose just three tricks.

(c) *The rebid over a new suit at the One level*

As noted in the last chapter, partner's response at the One level is wide ranging. Although the responder may be weak, he may also be strong and intending to go to game on the next round. Thus the first and invariable rule is that, unless responder has previously passed, opener must keep the bidding open.

There are three types of rebid that immediately limit the opener's hand. First is a simple rebid of his own suit. After 1D–1S you hold:

```
♠ 7
♡ Q 7 6 3
◇ K J 10 8 5 2
♣ A J
```

The obvious rebid is Two Diamonds. This means that your diamonds are rebiddable, probably a six-card suit, that you are not far from minimum, and that you lack support for spades.

The second limiting rebid is a single raise of partner's suit. Again after 1D–1S you hold:

```
♠ Q 10 7
♡ 5
◇ A Q 10 8 4
♣ A 9 6 2
```

Raise to Two Spades. The message is that you are not far from minimum but have support for spades.

Thirdly, opener can express a minimum hand by rebidding 1NT. Beginners may not wish to concern themselves with such niceties, but it must be said that most players make a distinction between a rebid of 1NT when vulnerable and when not vulnerable. If the *opening* 1NT is 12–14, then a rebid of 1NT suggests 15–16; if the opening 1NT is 15–17, then a rebid of 1NT suggests 12–14. This arrangement does in fact simplify the bidding of many hands.

We turn next to sequences that are encouraging but not forcing. First is the jump to 2NT.

South	North
1D	1H
2NT	

South's rebid suggests a hand in the 16–18 range; if 16, there should be a fair five-card suit. This would be typical:

♠ A 10 5
♡ J 2
◇ A K 8 6 3
♣ K Q 6

A *jump rebid* shows similar values:

South	North
1H	1S
3H	

South holds:

♠ K 2
♡ A Q 10 9 7 4
◇ K 9 6
♣ A 5

South, as you see, holds an Ace above a minimum opening and his hearts are strong. Note, however, that with similar values in a minor suit the opener should take the short route to game and rebid in notrumps. After 1D–1S South holds:

♠ 5 4
♡ A J
◇ A K 10 8 6 2
♣ A 9 6

Now 2NT is a more constructive rebid than Three Diamonds. With good support for partner's suit, opener may raise to the Three level. After 1C–1H you hold:

(1)	♠ K 8 4	(2)	♠ 5
	♡ A 8 6 2		♡ Q J 6 3
	◇ 3		◇ A 5
	♣ A K Q 7 3		♣ A K 8 6 4 2

In each case raise to Three Hearts. The second hand contains only 14 points, but it is strong in support of hearts.

A new suit of higher rank than the first suit is always encouraging.

South	*North*
1D	1S
2H	

By bidding Two Hearts on the second round, South forces his partner to go to the Three level if he has better diamonds than hearts. The sequence is called a *reverse*. This would be a minimum:

> ♠ 6 3
> ♡ A K 6 2
> ◇ A Q 10 8 5
> ♣ K 4

Apart from the reverse, a simple change of suit has a wide range, from about 12 to 18. When very strong, expecting to make game opposite a minimum response, opener may either bid game or jump in a new suit.

South	*North*	*South*	*North*
1D	1H	1D	1H
2S		3C	

In each case the jump in a new suit is unconditionally forcing to game. One reason why North must not pass is that the jump may conceal extremely strong support for hearts. For example, in the second sequence South may hold:

> ♠ 5
> ♡ K Q 6 4
> ◇ A K J 7 3
> ♣ A Q 2

South is too strong for a raise to Four Hearts and so forces in a non-existent suit.

(d) The rebid over a new suit at the Two level
The bidding begins:

South	North
1H	2C

South can limit his hand by a simple rebid in hearts.

There are, unfortunately, two ways of regarding a rebid of 2NT. Some players treat this as a constructive rebid, suggesting 15–17, others as a minimum 12–14. It is one of the points on which a partnership must agree. Either method is playable.

A raise to Three Clubs would be constructive but not forcing.

A rebid of Two Diamonds, though not technically forcing, would almost never be passed. This change of suit does not necessarily show additional values. The range is from about 12 to 17. If he is stronger, the opener can jump in a new suit; it must be said, however, that for many players such a jump implies support for the responder's suit.

The strength required for a jump to 3NT depends on whether 2NT is a minimum or a constructive rebid. If 2NT suggests 12–14, then 3NT may be bid on about 16–17, but if 2NT is stronger, then so is 3NT.

A reverse (1H–2C–2S) is forcing, and so is a new suit at the range of Three (1S–2D–3C).

(e) The rebid over 2NT
This response, it will be remembered, indicates a balanced hand in the 11–13 range. Opener should pass only with a balanced minimum.

With an unbalanced hand the opener may introduce a new suit. This is forcing for one round. The bidding goes:

South	North
1H	2NT
3C	

The new suit is forcing, but if responder can do no more than bid Three Hearts, opener is free to pass.

A repeat of opener's first suit at the Three level is generally played as a sign of weakness. After 1H–2NT South holds:

♠ K 5 2
♡ A 10 8 7 5 3
◇ K J 4
♣ 3

South bids Three Hearts, and responder is expected to pass unless he has undisclosed support for hearts.

(f) The rebid over a double raise

After a double raise in a major suit, 1H–3H, opener should go to game unless his hand is minimum in every way. A double raise in a minor suit is less compelling, to the extent that the responder will seldom have length in either major and will probably hold a singleton, which may be a handicap for notrumps.

(g) The rebid over a force

In general, the opener should rebid on natural lines, either repeating his first suit or bidding a second suit or bidding notrumps with a balanced hand. At this point, since the partnership is committed to game, opener shows his *type*, not his strength. The only time when opener may jump is when he holds a solid suit. The bidding begins:

South	North
1H	3D
?	

South holds:

♠ 5
♡ A K Q J 7 4
◇ 6 3 2
♣ Q 10 6

Now a jump to Four Hearts would say: 'I have a solid suit of hearts, requiring no support, but not much else.'

Test of opener's first rebid

You open One Heart and your partner responds 1NT. What do you rebid on the following hands?

1 ♠ K 7 6	2 ♠ 5	3 ♠ A 10 5
♡ A J 5 4 2	♡ A J 10 8 6 3	♡ A K Q 10 4
◇ K Q 3	◇ A 10 8 5	◇ K Q 3
♣ A 4	♣ A 5	♣ 10 6

Answers

1 2NT. Not more, with a flat 17.

2 3H. This is a strong hand for play in hearts.

3 3NT. Game is more likely in notrumps than in hearts.

You open One Spade and partner raises to Two Spades. What do you rebid on the following hands?

1 ♠ K Q J 4	2 ♠ K Q 9 6 4	3 ♠ A Q 10 8 3 2
♡ K 7 4	♡ A 3	♡ J 4
◇ A J 6 3	◇ A Q 10 8 6	◇ A Q 3
♣ Q 6	♣ 4	♣ K 5

Answers

1 Pass. Not worth a try, with a flat 16.

2 4S. This is a powerful hand once the spades have been supported; there is no point in mentioning the diamonds.

3 3S. A trial bid of 3D would not be a mistake, but by bidding Three of the trump suit you indicate that high cards in any side suit would be useful.

You open One Diamond and partner responds One Heart. What do you rebid on the following hands?

1 ♠ Q 4	2 ♠ K 10 6 3	3 ♠ A 6 4 2
♡ K 9 7	♡ J 4	♡ Q 7 6
◇ A Q J 5	◇ K Q 7 4	◇ A J 10 5 3
♣ A Q 3 2	♣ A 9 5	♣ 4

Answers

1 2NT. With 18 points you are too strong for 2H; your trump support is not good enough for 3H; 2NT expresses the values better than 2C.

2 1S. You should not, as a rule, by-pass a four-card suit that can be bid at the One level.

3 2H. You may, however, by-pass 1S when you are supporting the other major suit. If this hand were stronger – say with

H A instead of H Q – you could bid 1S and support hearts on the next round.

You open One Spade and partner responds Two Clubs. You are playing 2NT as a minimum rebid in this sequence. What do you rebid on the following hands?

1	♠ A J 9 7 4	2	♠ A Q 8 5 3	3	♠ K Q 10 7 2
	♡ 6 4		♡ 5 4		♡ A Q 9 5 3
	◊ A K 4		◊ A Q 6 2		◊ 4
	♣ K 10 5		♣ 10 7		♣ A 3

Answers

1 2D. There are more serious drawbacks to all the alternatives. You are too strong for 2NT, if this is played as a weak rebid; 3NT is unattractive on a minimum with a plain doubleton in hearts; 3C would not give a picture of the general strength.

2 2D. Although you have a minimum opening, you should not distort the hand by rebidding 2S.

3 2H. A promising hand, but there is no need to jump at this stage. Remember that a player who has responded at the Two level will almost always find another bid.

Test of responder's action on the second round

The bidding goes:

South	North
1D	1H
1S	?

As North, what do you rebid on the following hands?

1	♠ Q 5 3	2	♠ K 8 6 3	3	♠ K 5
	♡ A J 8 6 4		♡ K 9 7 4 3		♡ A 10 7 3
	◊ 10 6		◊ —		◊ K 8 4
	♣ J 8 4		♣ J 7 5 2		♣ K J 6 2

Answers

1 1NT. Although you lack a firm *guard* in the unbid suit, clubs, 1NT gives a more accurate picture of the values than 2S or 2H.

2 3S. The hand may look powerful opposite 1S, but partner's

second suit may not be strong and the void in his first suit is not an asset. However, you are closer to 4S than 2S.

3 3NT; no need to look elsewhere.

The bidding goes:

South	North
1S	2C
2H	?

As North, what do you rebid on the following hands?

1 ♠ 10 8 3
♡ K 2
◇ 7 4 3
♣ A K 6 4 2

2 ♠ 6 4
♡ 8 5 2
◇ Q 7
♣ A Q J 7 5 2

3 ♠ 9 5
♡ J 3
◇ Q 10 8 4
♣ A K 6 4 3

Answers

1 3S. This is *jump preference*. You cannot do less with the good fit in hearts.

2 3C. The opener may be quite strong, so you mustn't let the bidding die in 2H. By rebidding 3C you show long clubs in a moderate hand.

3 2NT. You are too good for 2S, which would be *simple preference*, and your holding in the unbid suit, diamonds, points to a rebid in notrumps.

8

The Strong Openings – 2NT,
Two of a Suit, Two Clubs

When you are the fortunate possessor of a hand that is outside the limits for a bid of One, you open with a bid at the Two level. This is a logical arrangement, because to open at a higher level would deprive your side of bidding space. An opening 2NT is not forcing; opening bids of Two Diamonds, Two Hearts and Two Spades are best played as forcing for one round; and Two Clubs is a conventional bid, unrelated to clubs, forcing to game in most sequences.

Opening 2NT and responses

2NT is not, as you might suppose, one step above 1NT. The range for a strong notrump is 15 to 17, or at most 16 to 18, but whatever the strength of your 1NT opening, the usual standard for 2NT is from a (good) 20 to 22. It is desirable, but not essential, to have a guard in all suits. These are typical openings:

(1) ♠ K 5
♡ A Q 10 7
◇ K J 5
♣ A K J 4

(2) ♠ A Q 5
♡ 10 7 4
◇ A K Q J 8
♣ A 10

(3) ♠ K Q 10 7 4
♡ A K 2
◇ Q 5
♣ A Q J

This is the scheme of responses to 2NT:

Pass	Less than 4 points and no suit length.
Three of a suit	Forcing. (It is possible to use 3C as an inquiry for four-card majors, but this is a matter for partnership agreement.)

4H or 4S	Long suit in an unbalanced hand, not a slam invitation.
3NT	Comparatively balanced, from about 4 to 10 points.

Partner opens 2NT and you hold:

(1)   ♠ 10 5
      ♡ 9 7 3 2
      ◇ K 8 6 4 2
      ♣ 5 3

(2)   ♠ 5 4 2
      ♡ Q 10 8 6 3
      ◇ 4
      ♣ A J 6 3

On (1) raise to 3NT, hoping that partner will be able to make use of your diamond suit. To bid Three Diamonds, a minor suit, would imply interest in going beyond 3NT. On (2) bid Three Hearts, which is forcing to game at least.

Opening Two Diamonds, Two Hearts and Two Spades

This is one of the many areas where you will need to have an understanding with your partner. The style I recommend here is that of the *Acol* system, where Two bids are forcing for one round. However, some players treat a Two bid as strong, but not forcing, while in the tournament world it is quite common to play weak Two bids in the majors – usually a six-card suit and about 6 to 10 points.

The forcing Two bid is useful on two types – powerful hands that lack the quality for Two Clubs (see next section) and strong two-suiters.

(1)   ♠ A Q J 10 6 3
      ♡ 5
      ◇ A K 6
      ♣ K J 6

(2)   ♠ A 4
      ♡ K Q J 8 6 3
      ◇ A Q 10 8 4
      ♣ —

The first hand is a typical one-suiter, the second a typical two-suiter. In each case you would be very unhappy if you opened with a bid One and everyone passed.

The weakness, or *negative*, response to an opening Two bid is 2NT. With a bad hand you may pass on the next round unless opener bids a new suit.

There are no fixed standards for a *positive* response. In general, you can respond more freely at the Two level than at the Three level. Partner opens Two Hearts and you hold:

(3) ♠ 5 3
    ♡ 6 2
    ◇ K Q 7 4 3
    ♣ J 9 6 2

(4) ♠ 6 4 2
    ♡ 9 6 5
    ◇ A 8 6 4 2
    ♣ J 3

On (3) you must begin with 2NT. If partner rebids Three Hearts, you raise to Four. On (2) you can raise Two Hearts to Three Hearts. Opposite a Two bid, three low trumps is adequate support. Many players demand an Ace for an immediate raise.

Opening Two Clubs and responses

In the early days of Contract Bridge any bid of Two in a suit was forcing to game. You have probably heard of the 'Culbertson' or 'Forcing Two' system. This is a very uneconomical style of bidding and it is much commoner nowadays to reserve Two Clubs for all hands from about 23 points upwards and some that contain fewer points but are of game-going quality.

(1) ♠ A K 8 6 4
    ♡ A K 10 5
    ◇ A J 4
    ♣ 6

(2) ♠ K Q 4
    ♡ A Q J 7
    ◇ A K 8
    ♣ A J 2

On (1) you cannot be sure of making a game opposite a blank hand, but one thing must be balanced against another and this represents a minimum Two Club opening. The second hand belongs to the type on which you would open Two Clubs and rebid 2NT over the negative response of Two Diamonds. The sequence 2C–2D–2NT suggests about 23 to 24 points and may be passed by a partner who has no long suit and fewer than 3 points.

Except when the rebid is 2NT, the opening Two Clubs is forcing to game. The traditional standard for a positive response (anything other than Two Diamonds) is an Ace and a King, or a K Q and a King, or three Kings; but these requirements need not be strictly observed when a good major suit is held.

Test of opening 2NT and responses

Your partner opens 2NT. What do you respond on the following hands?

1 ♠ K Q 8 6 2
♡ 5 4 2
♢ 10 3
♣ 8 7 4

2 ♠ 6
♡ J 9 7 6 4 2
♢ Q 6 4 3
♣ 5 4

3 ♠ A 4
♡ K J 8 5
♢ 6 3
♣ Q 10 8 5 4

Answers

1 3NT. It is unlikely that your side can make ten tricks in spades and only eight in notrumps, so you may as well play for game in notrumps. A response of 3S would encourage partner to raise to 4S.

2 4H. With this distribution there should be a play for game in hearts. Partner is warned not to advance.

3 3C. This is a strong hand opposite 2NT. Whether 3C is conventional or natural, it is the obvious response.

Test of opening two bids and responses

The bidding begins:

South	North
2H	2NT
3C	?

As North, what do you bid now on the following hands?

1 ♠ 6 5 4 2
♡ 3
♢ 10 8 6 5 4
♣ J 8 3

2 ♠ J 8 6 5
♡ 7 4 2
♢ A Q 3
♣ 10 6 2

3 ♠ Q 8 7 6 3
♡ 4 2
♢ J 8 6 4
♣ 5 3

Answers

1 3D. You are obliged to keep the bidding open after the change of suit, and the alternatives are worse. If partner bids simply 3H now, you can pass. If he repeats his clubs, you can raise to 5C.

2 4H. Holding an Ace and three trumps, you must not bid simply 3H. Remember that partner has opened a Two bid because he has hopes of game opposite a hand that is too weak to keep open a bid of One.

3 3H. After partner has bid two suits, it is unlikely that he will be interested in your spades. You should give him a chance to pass 3H.

Test of opening Two Clubs and responses

The bidding begins:

South	North
2C	2D
2S	?

As North, what do you bid on the following hands?

1 ♠ 5 4
♡ J 9 7 4 2
◇ 6 3
♣ 10 8 6 2

2 ♠ 7 4
♡ K 9 6 3
◇ Q J 8 4
♣ K 10 7

3 ♠ 8 6 4 2
♡ 7 4
◇ J 6 5
♣ 7 6 4 3

Answers

1 3H. When partner opens 2C he is marked with a high point count, but his own first suit may not be particularly strong. It is quite possible that your bid of 3H will enable him either to bid notrumps or to raise to game in hearts.

2 3NT, taking the opportunity to show that you have values in all three unbid suits.

3 2NT. On such a poor hand it is advisable to give a second negative and support spades on the next round. With an extra King you would raise at once to 3S.

9

Opening Bids of Three and Four

The time to open with a bid of Three or Four is when you hold a long suit and hope to buy the contract before the opponents have had a chance to exchange information. They are known as *pre-emptive* bids. Vulnerability must be taken into account, because when you open with a bid of this kind you expect to incur a penalty.

Opening Three bids and responses

It is necessary first to do a little calculation. Suppose that as dealer, not vulnerable, you hold:

♠ K Q J 10 7 6 3
♡ 5 4
♢ J 6
♣ 4 3

You would not think of opening One Spade on this hand, but you may open Three Spades. Suppose you are doubled and partner does not contribute a trick. The odds are that you will still make six tricks. Three down doubled, not vulnerable, costs 500. On this occasion you will score 100 for honours, so your net loss is 400. This is very far from being a disaster, because you will be saving an adverse game worth at least 400 to the opponents. (It is true that for, say, Four Hearts they would enter only 120 or 150, but the game has an unseen value because it takes them half-way to the rubber.) You may, indeed, be saving a slam, worth about 1000. In this case you will have obtained a very good bargain.

It happens more often, when you make this type of opening, that partner will hold some tricks and that you will be only one or two down, still saving a game. Quite often, too, the opponents will compete. Starting at a high level, they may well fail to arrive at their best contract.

Opening Three bids are frequently made on hands much less reliable than the one above. In a favourable situation, such as first or third in hand, not vulnerable, players open with a Three bid on hands of this type:

(1)   ♠ 5
      ♡ 7 2
      ◊ K J 10 7 6 4 3
      ♣ 5 3 2

(2)   ♠ 7 3
      ♡ K Q 10 8 7 4
      ◊ J 8 6 4 3
      ♣ —

Many writers will tell you that it is wrong to open with a pre-emptive bid on a semi-two-suiter such as hand (2), because the hand might play well in another denomination. This argument may have some force when the side suit is a major, but I can assure you that experienced players observe no such restrictions. Opponents who contest against such opening bids often run into very bad distribution.

When you are vulnerable you need to be rather more circumspect, because three down doubled is 800 – more than a game is worth to the opposition. Still, at game all, to lose 800, saving about 650, is not a calamity.

In first or second position at the table you should not open with a Three bid on any hand that would qualify for an opening bid of One. The main reason is that your partner expects you to be weak and may pass when your side could easily make a game.

In third position you may sometimes open with a pre-empt on a stronger hand such as:

(3)   ♠ 6 2
      ♡ A K J 10 7 3
      ◊ K 6 2
      ♣ 6 5

Since partner has passed, it is not likely that you will be missing a game if you open Three Hearts, and you may well create a problem for the next player.

In fourth position, after three passes, the possibility of shutting out the opponents obviously does not arise. An opening Three bid is still comparatively weak. It would be a sensible move on hand (3) above. You are not inviting partner to bid game, but you hope to snatch a part score.

Responding to Three bids

To make game opposite a weak Three bid, you need a minimum 14 points made up of top cards, especially Aces. Your partner opens Three Hearts as dealer, not vulnerable, the next player passes, and you hold:

(1)	♠ K J 5	(2)	♠ A 8
	♡ 6 4		♡ 5 2
	◇ A Q 7 3		◇ A Q 8 6 4 2
	♣ Q J 6 5		♣ K 6 2

To respond on (1) would be a bad mistake; the odds are that partner will fail to make even Three Hearts. The second hand is borderline. You would be more inclined to raise if partner were vulnerable.

Opening Four bids

An opening bid of Four in any suit is also pre-emptive, but you need reasonably good insurance against a heavy defeat, because opponents are much more likely to double you in a game bid of Four Hearts or Four Spades than in a part-score contract. Suppose you hold as dealer:

♠ 6 3
♡ K Q 9 8 7 5 3 2
◇ 5 4
♣ 6

Not vulnerable, you can certainly open Four Hearts. Vulnerable, you might run into a big penalty, but most players, holding seven likely tricks, would take the risk and open Four Hearts rather than Three Hearts.

On some hands the risk may be of a different kind – that by opening with a pre-emptive bid you may miss a slam. Suppose you hold:

♠ A K J 9 8 7 4
♡ 5
♢ K J 5 2
♣ 3

First or second in hand, you should open One Spade. In third or fourth hand, partner having passed, the danger of missing a slam is much smaller and it would be sensible to open Four Spades. The disadvantage of opening One Spade is that the opponents might find a fit in hearts or clubs and arrive at a profitable *sacrifice*.

Opening 3NT

An opening bid of 3NT is a special case. On the surface, it should mean a hand somewhat stronger than is required for an opening 2NT (20–22). As we have noted, however, balanced hands with 23–24 points are expressed by the sequence 2C–2D–2NT, and 2C–2D–3NT is available for the rare hands of 25 or more.

Consequently, players who use Two Clubs as a conventional opening on strong hands, tend to use 3NT in a special sense. The bid shows a solid minor suit and little side strength, such as:

♠ 5
♡ 6 3
♢ A K Q 10 8 6 2
♣ J 7 4

Partner, knowing that you have this type of hand, can always take out into Four Clubs. When your suit is diamonds, as in the present case, you will transfer to Four Diamonds.

I hesitate to recommend a convention of this type to inexperienced players. I say only that the convention is well known and that you must be prepared for it when you play in more sophisticated company.

Test of pre-emptive openings

As dealer, vulnerable, what do you open on the following hands?

1 ♠ A 8
  ♡ Q J 7 6 4 3 2
  ◇ 10 6
  ♣ 8 4

2 ♠ —
  ♡ 4 2
  ◇ K J 10 9 7 6 5 3
  ♣ Q 10 4

3 ♠ 5
  ♡ A Q J 10 8 6 2
  ◇ K Q 4
  ♣ Q 4

Answers

1 Pass. It is risky to open with a minimum pre-empt when your trump suit is not strong.

2 4D. You could lose 800 in this contract, but on balance you should be willing to stir things up. It is an advantage to be dealer and to get your blow in first.

3 1H. The hand contains too many high cards for a pre-empt of Four Hearts, though on occasions this call might turn out well.

Test of responses to opening Three bids

Your partner opens Three Hearts, not vulnerable, and the next player passes. What do you respond on the following hands?

1 ♠ J 4
  ♡ 5 3
  ◇ A K J 7 5 4
  ♣ K 7 6

2 ♠ A Q J 3
  ♡ 4
  ◇ K Q 8 4
  ♣ A J 8 3

3 ♠ 5 2
  ♡ K 8 6
  ◇ J 8 6 4 2
  ♣ A 4 3

Answers

1 Pass. You do not have enough for a raise to 4H and it would be foolish to fight partner with a bid of 4D. Any response in a new suit is forcing.

2 4H. It is true that if you were to bid 3NT most partners would go back to 4H, but an intelligent partner might not. With only a singleton heart you should not aim to play in notrumps, because you might have difficulty in establishing and running the long hearts.

3 4H. This is a tactical move. You don't expect to make 4H, but if you pass, the opponents are likely to compete, and undoubtedly they could make at least a part score, probably a game. By bidding 4H you may snatch the contract cheaply. If the opposing strength is divided you may not even be doubled.

IO

Slam Bidding

When the subject of slam bidding arises in an elementary book, I think of the harassed parent who says to the *au pair* 'Go and see what the children are doing and tell them they mustn't.' The point of this remark is that even the best players make several mistakes in the slam area. The sensible course for less experienced players is to bid the obvious ones and leave the rest alone. First, it is advisable to understand the mathematics of slam bidding.

The mathematics of slam bidding

The bonus for a non-vulnerable slam is 500. If you go one down you lose just 50 on the scoresheet, but meanwhile you have lost the opportunity for an easy game, worth about 450. Thus you want the slam to be even money. The cost of failure equals the reward for success.

When both sides are vulnerable, the calculation is easy. The bonus for a small slam is 750, but if you go one down you lose a penalty of 100 plus the value of the rubber game, about 650. So again you want even money. The best moment for a slam venture, though the difference is not great, is when your side is vulnerable and the opponents are not.

Grand slams are a different affair. For example, the bonus is 1000 not vulnerable, but if you go one down you have thrown away (assuming you could have made a small slam) 500 for slam plus a game equity of about 400 plus a trick score of about 180 – a total of 1080. Since the grand slam brings in an *extra* 500 only, you need odds of more than 2 to 1 in favour. This means that you want to be fairly sure of your ground before abandoning a safe small slam in pursuit of a grand slam.

These figures are not important, and the only reason why I give them is to point the folly of players who go for an unlikely slam and say, 'It only cost 50.'

How to recognise when a slam is likely

The easiest slams to reach are those where you have such a weight of high cards that simple arithmetic will show you are in the slam zone. Suppose that partner opens a strong notrump, 15–17, and you hold a balanced 18. A total of 33 will normally provide a play for Six, even without a long suit, so you know at once that 6NT is a strong possibility.

However, it is seldom as easy as that. The great majority of slams depend on long suits and distributional features. Until you gain experience, this is a fair test to apply:

If you could take an Ace away from your hand and still be confident of game, there should be slam possibilities.

We will look briefly at one or two examples where this test can be usefully applied.

```
         West              East
    ♠ A K 9 6 3        ♠ 8
    ♡ Q 10 7 5         ♡ A J 9 8 4 3
    ♦ A 7 4            ♦ K 6 5
    ♣ 6               ♣ A 10 7
```

West opens One Spade, East responds Two Hearts, and West, with four trumps and good distribution, raises to Four Hearts. Take the Ace of clubs away from East, and he would still expect to make Four Hearts, as the bidding has gone. He is therefore in the slam zone. Note that in high cards the two hands contain only 25 points between them. However, the hands fit well, and Seven is on a finesse. (East can discard a diamond on the high spades and can ruff his two losing clubs.)

	West	*East*
♠	J 6	A K 10 9 7 2
♡	A Q 8	5 3
◇	A K 9 6 2	J 4
♣	K 10 4	A J 6

The bidding begins:

West	*East*
1D	1S
2NT	?

West's rebid shows about 17 points. East would be confident of game with an Ace less than he holds, so again he can investigate a slam. Six Spades might fail on a heart lead from South, but it would be a reasonable contract.

	West	*East*
♠	K Q 10 6	A 9 5 2
♡	5 3	A Q 7 5 3
◇	A 8	Q 8 5
♣	A K J 7 3	4

The bidding begins:

West	*East*
1C	1H
1S	4S
?	

West would have bid in the same way up to now with an Ace less, so he can think about a small slam.

The next question is what steps to take when a small slam seems to be on the horizon.

How to approach a slam

There are various ways of inviting a slam. An obvious way is to carry the bidding beyond game, following a sequence such as 2NT–4NT. As a rule, however, it is necessary to check on *controls*. This is a complicated affair, and we will look at simple examples only.

When a trump suit has been clearly agreed, a new suit at the Four level is a *cue bid*, usually denoting first-round control. The bidding goes:

West	East
1D	1S
3S	4H

East's bid of Four Hearts is not an attempt to find a new suit. He is saying, 'After your opening bid and double raise I think there may be a slam. I have a control in hearts.' Control in this context usually means Ace or void, but sometimes it may be only a second-round control – King or singleton. In the present sequence East might hold:

♠ A Q J 8 5
♡ K Q 3
♢ Q J 4
♣ 6 2

The best slam try available over Three Spades is Four Hearts. If East had held a control in clubs he would have bid this lower control first, so in addition to showing the heart control Four Hearts denies a control in clubs.

Sometimes an exchange of cue bids will indicate that control of a particular suit is missing. West and East hold:

West	East
♠ K J 10 4	♠ A Q 9 6 5
♡ A K J 9 3	♡ Q 6
♢ Q 7 2	♢ 8 3
♣ J	♣ A K 10 5

The bidding begins:

West	East
1H	1S
3S	4C
4H	?

East's Four Clubs is a cue bid and so, although it is not a new suit, is West's Four Hearts. Since his partner has by-passed the diamonds, East will realise that there are two losers in diamonds. He will therefore bid only Four Spades over Four Hearts.

Blackwood

There are also ways of showing a number of Aces in a single bid. You have probably heard of the *Blackwood convention*, much loved by a certain class of player. When this convention is played, a bid of 4NT, if not a straightforward raise in no-trumps, asks the responder to declare the number of Aces he holds. This is the usual pattern:

With 0 or 4 Aces	5C
With 1 Ace	5D
With two Aces	5H
With three Aces	5S

A bid of 5NT on the next round asks for Kings to be shown according to a similar pattern.

This convention has a deceptive simplicity and is over-used. Most slams do not depend on Aces alone but on a variety of good features, such as a sixth trump, an odd Queen, or a singleton in the right place. Also, the knowledge of how many Aces are held does not necessarily solve the important problems. Look again at the last hand we discussed:

West	*East*
♠ K J 10 4	♠ A Q 9 6 5
♡ A K J 9 3	♡ Q 6
◇ Q 7 2	◇ 8 3
♣ J	♣ A K 10 5

The bidding begins:

West	*East*
1H	1S
3S	?

If East, a Blackwood addict, bids 4NT now (instead of making a cue bid in clubs), he learns, from the response of Five Diamonds, that his partner holds one Ace. He still doesn't know whether or not there are two losing diamonds.

The time to use Blackwood is when you possess the general values for a slam but need to be sure that two Aces are not missing. Do not say to yourself 'If partner has (say) two Aces we can make a slam.' You must be able to say, instead, 'Unless partner is short of Aces, a slam must be on.' There *is* a difference.

Finally, it is important to realise that slam bidding is not a separate art. It is just an extension of earlier bidding. Do not, therefore, spend time on learning various slam conventions. They will be useless unless the early bidding is well constructed.

I I

The Scoring

We have completed our review of constructive bidding, and it is time now to examine the scoring, because this is very relevant to defensive and competitive bidding.

A scoresheet for Rubber Bridge has two columns and a heavy line across the centre. All players should keep the score, entering their own scores in the left-hand column. Few things are more annoying than to have a partner who makes a series of mistakes in bidding because he doesn't known the part-score position. Indulgence would be granted to a novice, but it is incorrect to draw partner's attention to the score once he has picked up his cards.

Scores below the line

We have already noted the scoring below the line. The various denominations have the following values:

Notrumps: first trick, 40; each subsequent trick, 30.
Spades and hearts: each trick, 30.
Diamonds and clubs: each trick, 20.

When you have made a game (100 or more), you draw a line below, and previous part scores are cancelled, in the sense that they no longer contribute to game.

When only a part score is made, the overtricks (unless the part score produces a game) must be entered above the line. Thus 2NT bid, Three made, is scored as 70 below and 30 above. But when game has been made, as in Four Spades bid, Five made, it is normal to enter 150 below.

When a contract has been doubled and made, the trick score is doubled and entered below the line in the usual way. Thus Three Diamonds doubled is entered as 120 below. As we will see in a moment, there is also a bonus, which technically belongs above the line.

When a contract has been redoubled and made, the trick score is multiplied by four.

Bonuses for doubled contracts

In addition to all other scores, there is a bonus of 50 for any doubled or redoubled contract made.

Not vulnerable, overtricks in doubled contracts count 100 each. Vulnerable, each overtrick counts 200. When the contract has been redoubled, these totals are doubled.

Examples: Four Hearts doubled, Five made, not vulnerable, scores 240 below the line, 50 for the 'insult', as it is often called, 100 for the overtrick.

2NT redoubled, vulnerable, Four made, would be 280 below, 50 for the insult, 800 for the two overtricks, plus 500 or 700 for the rubber. Not a likely happening, be it said!

Slam bonuses, honours, rubber bonus

Small slam not vulnerable scores 500; vulnerable, 750.

Grand slam not vulnerable scores 1000; vulnerable, 1500.

Any player who holds four honours in the trump suit scores 100. Any player who holds five honours in the trump suit scores 150. Any player who holds four Aces in a notrump contract scores 150.

Rubber bonus: when the rubber is won by two games to none, 700; when the rubber is won by two games to one, 500. If for any reason a rubber cannot be finished, a side that is game up scores 300; a side that has a part score in an uncompleted game scores 50.

Penalties for Undertricks

Not vulnerable, undoubled, there is a penalty of 50 for each undertrick; vulnerable, 100 for each undertrick.

Not vulnerable, doubled, the penalty for the first undertrick is 100, for each subsequent undertrick 200.

Vulnerable, doubled, the penalty for the first undertrick is 200, for each subsequent undertrick 300.

Examples: two down doubled, not vulnerable, is 300; three down doubled, vulnerable, is 800.

12

Defensive Overcalls

We turn now to action by the defending side. Broadly speaking, a defender who overcalls in a suit has a different objective from a player who opens the bidding. A player who opens, say, One Club is making the first move towards what he hopes will eventually be a game or slam contract. A player who overcalls One Club with, say, One Spade, is not thinking so much about reaching a game contract (though it may turn out that way) as about making it difficult for the opponents to reach, and achieve, *their* best contract. With this in mind, we look first at simple overcalls of One in a suit.

An overcall of One in a suit

When overcalling, high cards are not as important as playing strength. Suppose the opponent on your right opens One Club at love all and in second position you hold:

♠ K Q 9 7 6 3
♡ 5 4
♢ Q 7 6 3
♣ 2

You would not open the bidding on this hand, of course, but there are advantages in overcalling with One Spade. That you will reach, and make, a high contract in spades is unlikely, though not impossible. But you may incommode the opponents in various ways. You may stop them from reaching 3NT; you may arrive at a profitable sacrifice of Four Spades over 3NT or Four Hearts; you suggest a good attack to your partner, should he make the opening lead; and to a limited extent you deprive the opponents of bidding space. For example, the next player can no longer make a One-over-One response of One Heart or One Diamond.

Points are not important, but the general range for an overcall at the One level, not vulnerable, is from about 6 to 14. Vulnerable, the lower limit is more like 8 or 9, because partner will take a vulnerable overcall more seriously. Even so, it is not wrong to overcall on a strong suit such as A Q J 9 x x, with no outside strength.

Overcalls on hands that contain high cards but no good suit are less attractive. Suppose, again, that the opponent on your right, at game all, opens One Heart and you hold:

♠ A Q 6 3
♡ Q 10 6 2
♢ 4 3
♣ K 7 3

To overcall with One Spade would be wrong for several reasons. The suit is poor; the hand is strong in defence against hearts; and by bidding One Spade you do not deprive the opponents of bidding space. You should pass and see how the bidding develops.

An overcall of Two of a suit

At the Two level you are much more likely to run into a penalty double. A fairly strong suit is essential. The bidding is opened on your right with One Heart at game all and you hold:

(1) ♠ A J 5   (2) ♠ A 5
   ♡ Q 10 8   ♡ 7 4 2
   ♢ A J 7 5 3   ♢ J 3
   ♣ 6 4   ♣ K Q 10 9 6 2

On the first hand you might overcall with Two Diamonds if your opponents were 60 up, but to overcall at any other time would be dangerous and unlikely to achieve anything. The second hand represents a minimum overcall at the Two level.

Jump overcalls and 1NT overcall

An overcall of one range higher than necessary is a *jump overcall*. Vulnerability makes a difference, but in general a jump overcall suggests a better than minimum opening bid with a good six-card suit. With neither side vulnerable the player on your right opens One Heart and you hold:

(1) ♠ A Q J 9 8 3 (2) ♠ 7 6
    ♡ 5   ♡ 5 3
    ◇ A J 10 8   ◇ A Q 4
    ♣ Q 4   ♣ A K J 10 8 4

On (1) you could bid Two Spades, and on (2) Three Clubs.

An overcall of 1NT is very much exposed to the elements. Not vulnerable, you need about 15 to 17, preferably with a suit on which you can play, as well as a guard in the opponent's suit. Vulnerable, you need about 17 to 18 – or 16 with a fair suit. At love all there is an opening bid of One Spade on your right and you hold:

(3) ♠ A 8 5   (4) ♠ K J 4
    ♡ K J 5   ♡ A 5
    ◇ A 8 7 3   ◇ K Q J 9 3
    ♣ Q 6 4   ♣ J 10 8

Hand (3) is the worst possible type for an overcall of 1NT. You have only one stop in spades and no suit to develop. The second hand is far stronger, and 1NT is a better bid than Two Diamonds.

Overcalls in the protective position

When an opening bid is followed by two passes, the fourth player may *protect* on less than is required for an immediate overcall. Say that the bidding begins:

South	West	North	East
1S	No	No	?

East holds:

(1) ♠ 5 4   (2) ♠ J 7 4
    ♡ 7 2   ♡ A 10 8
    ◇ A Q 8 5 3   ◇ K 9 7 3
    ♣ K 6 4 2   ♣ K Q 6

Vulnerable or not, East can protect with Two Diamonds on
(1) and with 1NT on (2). The average strength for 1NT in the
protective position is 11 to 14 and a firm guard in the opponent's
suit is not altogether necessary. Bidding in this position, you
are much less exposed to a penalty double than when overcalling
in front of a player who has heard his partner open.

Oddly enough, it may be quite sound, when the bidding
would otherwise die, to protect at the Two level on a hand that
did not justify an overcall at the One level. The bidding goes:

South	West	North	East
1D	No	1H	No
2H	No	No	?

East holds:

(3) ♠ K J 8 6 3
     ♡ 7 5 4
     ♢ 4 2
     ♣ A 8 5

There are various reasons why you may now protect with Two
Spades, even though it was right not to intervene with One
Spade on the previous round. Since opponents have died in Two
Hearts, it is certain that partner has some values. In all probability West has diamond strength over the opening bidder; that is
why he passed on the first round. The fact that you have three
hearts, the suit bid and supported against you, is a favourable
sign; partner is probably short in hearts and may therefore hold
some support for spades. Finally, it is wrong to take the view
that 'they will not get far in Two Hearts'. To challenge in the
part-score area is most important.

Responding to overcalls

The defenders do not, as a rule, have space in which to make
the kind of delicate approach bids that are practised by the opening bidder and the responder. Simple changes of suit are not
forcing. The only way to make a forcing bid is to bid the opponent's suit. Since reasonably good suits are required for overcalls, especially at the Two level, players should be disposed if

possible to support their partners. At game all the bidding begins:

South	West	North	East
1S	2H	No	?

East holds:

(1) ♠ 10 5　　　　　　(2) ♠ K 9 7
　　♡ Q 3　　　　　　　　♡ 10 4
　　◇ A Q 8 6 3 2　　　　◇ A Q 6 3
　　♣ K J 3　　　　　　　♣ Q 10 7 4

On (1) East should support his partner's hearts. He has ample for Three Hearts and with some partners it would be safe to bid Four. Remember that Three Diamonds would not be forcing. On (2) East, facing a vulnerable overcall at the Two level, has enough for 2NT.

When the responder is strong, but cannot bid game directly, he can force by bidding the opponent's suit. This bid is commonly used in two senses. The bidding begins:

South	West	North	East
1S	2D	No	?

East holds:

(3) ♠ 4　　　　　　　(4) ♠ 6 4
　　♡ A 6 4　　　　　　　♡ A K 5 4
　　◇ K 10 8 5　　　　　　◇ K 7 4
　　♣ A K Q 6 3　　　　　♣ Q 8 6 2

On (3) East will always go to Five Diamonds eventually, and a slam is quite likely. For the moment he bids Two Spades. On the second hand the most likely game is in notrumps. Again, East will bid Two Spades. If West has a spade guard he may well rebid in notrumps, and East can raise. The bid of the opponent's suit was at one time considered forcing to game, but among experienced players it is used freely by both the opening side and the defending side as a general-purpose force. On the present hand East would pass a rebid of Three Diamonds.

Test of overcalls

At love all, the player on your right opens One Heart. What is your action with the following hands?

1 ♠ K 3	2 ♠ A 10 8 6 2	3 ♠ K 9 4
♡ 9 7 4 2	♡ 6 3 2	♡ A Q 10 8
◇ A K J 3	◇ 5	◇ A 7 5 3
♣ 6 4 2	♣ K 9 6 4	♣ 6 2

Answers

1 Pass. You have a defensive type and it is unsound to overcall at the Two level on a four-card suit.

2 1S. Not a great hand, but it could play well in spades and partner will not carry you too high after a non-vulnerable overcall at the One level.

3 Pass. This is generally the best tactical move when your main strength is in the opponent's suit.

You are vulnerable, the opponents are not, and the bidding goes:

South	West	North	East
1D	1S	No	?

As East, what action do you take on the following hands?

1 ♠ 4	2 ♠ Q 7 4	3 ♠ A 8
♡ A 5 2	♡ 5	♡ 7 4 3
◇ Q 8 7 6 4 2	◇ A 8 7 4	◇ K 10 7 6
♣ 6 4 3	♣ K 6 4 3 2	♣ Q 8 5 4

Answers

1 Pass. You should not 'take out on weakness'. Partner is as likely to make 1S as you are to make 2D. Also, he may advance over 2D.

2 3S. This is a sound raise on your values.

3 1NT. It would not be a mistake to pass, but you have a strong guard in diamonds and want to avoid a lead through the King.

13

Penalty and Take-out Doubles

As mentioned in Chapter 1, doubles are not always what they seem. In a great many situations a double is a sign of general strength, not an attempt to penalise the opponents. The so-called *take-out double* is a convention, but so familiar to Bridge players that they scarcely think of it in that way. It is amusing to reflect that when take-out doubles (then called 'informatory' doubles) were introduced into Auction Bridge in about 1920, some writers violently abused players who presumed to use such artificiality. If only it had stopped there! Needless to say, it is highly important to distinguish between the two types of double.

Distinguishing between penalty and take–out doubles

In general, a take-out double asks partner to indicate where his strength lies. Consequently, any double made *after* partner has declared himself in any positive direction is a penalty double, made with the expectation of defeating the contract.

(1) *South*	*West*	*North*	*East*
1H	2D	dble	

(2) *South*	*West*	*North*	*East*
1H	No	No	dble
No	No	1NT	dble

In the first sequence North's double is obviously for penalties, because South has made a positive bid of One Heart. In the second sequence West has passed twice, but his second pass was a *penalty pass*, indicating a desire to defend against One Heart doubled. West has therefore declared where his strength lies, and East's double of 1NT is a penalty double.

A double of an opening 1NT is also a penalty double in principle. We discuss the requirements in the next section.

When partner has not made a bid (or a penalty pass), a double of One or Two in a suit, and often a double at the Three level also, is for take-out if made at the first opportunity of doubling.

(3)	South	West	North	East
	1H	dble	1S	dble

West's double is for take-out; East's for penalties, because his partner has already shown strength.

(4)	South	West	North	East
	1C	1H	No	2H
	dble			

A player who has opened the bidding, and whose partner has so far passed, will often double for take-out.

(5)	South	West	North	East
	1H	No	1NT	No
	2H	dble		

This is a penalty double; West had the opportunity to double One Heart for take-out on the previous round.

(6)	South	West	North	East
	1D	No	1S	No
	2D	No	No	dble

No definition takes care of all doubling situations. Here it is true that West has not made a bid of any kind, but the double is still for take-out. East is in the protective position and, when Two Diamonds is passed by North, he may be able to judge that his side has the balance of the cards. It is very unlikely that, sitting under the bidder, he would want to double for penalties.

(7)	South	West	North	East
	1C	No	3C	dble

A double at the Three level, when opponents have found a fit, is for take-out. If the opponents are evidently struggling, then a double at this level will be for penalties.

Doubling for penalties

This area is so diversified and depends to such an extent on individual circumstances that it is possible to make only a few general observations.

Doubling at a low level

Many of the most rewarding doubles occur at low levels, generally the Two level. Trump strength is desirable but it is not everything. The bidding begins:

South	West	North	East
1S	2D	?	

North holds:

(1) ♠ 5
♡ A 7 6 2
♢ K 7 5
♣ Q 9 6 4 3

(2) ♠ Q 7 6
♡ 4 2
♢ K J 9 5 3 2
♣ J 8

Of the two hands, (1) is the better double. You have a singleton of your partner's suit to lead and will, in all probability, obtain a spade ruff. It is not a cast-iron double, but if the opponents make Two Diamonds doubled it will not give them game. On the second hand you may think you will kill them in Two Diamonds, but you could easily be disappointed. For one thing, it is a disadvantage to hold length in your partner's suit; it may well mean that his high cards will be wasted, since they will be ruffed. Secondly, you may find in the play that your great length in trumps will become a liability. The declarer will make what tricks he can in the side suits and with his own low trumps, and you will find eventually that you will be forced to lead trumps into his strong holding. It is true that your partner, who may be void of diamonds, may remove the double, and that you can stand Two Spades. The point I want to make is simply that great length in the trump suit can be an illusion.

Doubling at game level

There are two points to be made about doubles at game level. The first is that the mathematics of scoring are heavily weighted against the doubler. Suppose you double the opponents in Four Spades not vulnerable. If they make the contract they score an *extra* 170 (240 below and 50 for the insult instead of 120). If you get them one down you score only an *extra* 50. So, when the issue is likely to be close, you are laying 7 to 2 on your being right. It is silly, therefore, to double simply because you have been outbid.

Secondly, the best reason for doubling opponents in a contract they have reached voluntarily is that your hand contains an unpleasant surprise for them. Obviously, if you hold Q J 10 8 in the trump suit, you will make tricks they will not have expected to lose. If you hold a singleton in a side suit which they have bid and supported, then probably your partner will hold a trick in this suit. But if you hold, say, two Aces and a K Q, this is *nothing*. Respect the opponents' intelligence to the point of assuming that they *know* they do not hold these cards and have strong distribution to compensate.

Double of 1NT

Next, beware of doubling an opponent's 1NT because you, too, hold a good balanced hand. South, playing a weak notrump, opens 1NT and in second position you hold:

$$
\begin{array}{ll}
\spadesuit & \text{K 10 5} \\
\heartsuit & \text{Q 9 6 3} \\
\diamondsuit & \text{A J 4} \\
\clubsuit & \text{K J 3}
\end{array}
$$

Do not consider a double. If North holds a few points he may pass, in which case they will make 1NT doubled with overtricks, or he may redouble and obtain a penalty of 300 or more from any rescue that your side may attempt.

To double 1NT, you should hold at least two points more than the average of the player whom you are doubling, and it may be very important to have a good lead. In general, it is more dangerous to double 1NT in fourth position, after two passes, than in second position. This is because you cannot rely on a favourable lead.

Doubling a slam

Finally, a special convention, known as the *Lightner slam double*, applies to doubles of freely bid slam contracts. Suppose that opponents bid to Six Hearts after your side has overcalled in clubs. Your partner, who is not on lead, doubles the final contract. He is saying, 'Make an *unexpected* lead: not the obvious club, and not a trump.' You will have to work out what he wants. Usually it is not difficult; he may be void of a suit that has not been mentioned by either side. I do not suggest that, in a game for beginners, you should make Lightner doubles or interpret your partner's double in that sense; but the convention is so well known, and so obviously useful, that you should be familiar with it.

The requirements for a take-out double

The most important, though by no means the only, occasion for a take-out double is when the bidding has been opened on your right. If you have a fair hand, shortage in the suit bid, and can cope with any response that partner may make, you may begin a counter-attack by doubling. South opens One Diamond and West holds:

(1)		(2)	
♠	K 9 7 5 2	♠	K 4
♡	A J 8 4	♡	A 9 6 3
◇	5	◇	K 8 4
♣	Q 10 3	♣	K 6 3 2

On (1) your point count is low for a double, but you have good *preparedness* for both majors. You have a minimum distributional double. The second hand is stronger in high cards but the support for spades is poor. On this hand it would be wiser to pass.

With a strong hand, upwards of 15 points, you should be more inclined to double than to make a simple overcall. South opens One Club and West holds:

(3)		(4)	
♠	A 10 7 4	♠	5
♡	A K 8 6 3	♡	A Q 10 6 3
◇	4 2	◇	A K J 4
♣	A 9	♣	Q 6 2

On (3) you lack support for diamonds, but if partner responds in diamonds you can bid your hearts. Hand (4) is awkward, because you lack support for one of the major suits, and your hearts do not justify a jump overcall. The sensible course is to bid simply One Heart and hope that the bidding will not die.

With a very strong hand you may consider an immediate overcall in the opponent's suit. Over an opening One Heart you hold:

(5) ♠ A Q J 6   (6) ♠ A K J 8 7
     ♡ —   ♡ 4
     ◇ A K 8 6 3   ◇ A K J 9 8 3
     ♣ A Q 5 4   ♣ 5

On both hands overcall with Two Hearts. This is forcing for at least two rounds.

Responding to a take-out double

The bidding begins:

South	West	North	East
1D	dble	No	?

The one thing that East must *not* do is pass on a bad hand. The result may well be that the opponents will make One Diamond doubled, with overtricks, while your partner could have made at least a part score in his own suit. The only time when East may pass is when his trumps are so strong that he can expect to make at least three, probably four, tricks in the trump suit itself, a hand such as:

Apart from the penalty pass, this is the scheme for East:

- (*a*) On a weak, or moderate, hand respond in his best suit at minimum level.
- (*b*) With some strength in the opponent's suit and no four-card major, bid 1NT.
- (*c*) With a fair hand, about 8 to 10 points, jump in his best suit. This is not forcing.

(*d*) With a good hand and a satisfactory suit, go straight to game. With no good suit, respond in the opponent's suit. This puts the ball back into partner's court. A responder who makes a cue bid of this kind undertakes to bid again.

(*e*) If third hand bids over the double, East has additional options: to pass with a poor hand or to double for penalties.

At game all the bidding begins:

South	West	North	East
1H	dble	No	?

East holds:

(1) ♠ 6 4
♡ K J 7 5 3
♢ Q 6 3 2
♣ 5 4

(2) ♠ J 7 5 3
♡ 6 4
♢ Q 9 7 5 3
♣ J 4

On (1) bid 1NT. Do not consider passing. On (2) bid One Spade rather than Two Diamonds. A player who doubles one major will almost always be strong in the other major.

After the same beginning East holds:

(3) ♠ 7 5 3
♡ Q 8 6 2
♢ 6 4 3
♣ 10 6 5

(4) ♠ Q 10 8 5 3
♡ 7 4 2
♢ A J 9 5
♣ 4

On (3) you must not pass, and 1NT should be avoided on very weak hands. Many players would respond One Spade, on the grounds that it was the cheapest bid available. So it may be for the moment, but it could prove very expensive should partner innocently support spades. The best that East can do in this parlous situation is respond Two Clubs. Hand (4) justifies a non-forcing jump to Two Spades.

Action by third hand over a double

The bidding begins:

South	West	North	East
1S	dble	?	

There are different theories about the action by third hand over a double. The traditional scheme is on the following lines:

   (a) With a fair to moderate hand, bid a good suit, but not a short suit, because changes of suit are not forcing in this sequence. A jump response is similarly non-forcing.

   (b) With support for his partner's suit, raise to the limit, usually to a level higher than if there had been no double.

   (c) With a strong hand, redouble.

After the sequence shown above, North holds:

   (1) ♠ 8   (2) ♠ J 9 7 4
       ♡ J 7 5 3   ♡ 6 3
       ◇ A Q 10 7 4 2   ◇ 5 4
       ♣ 5 4   ♣ A 7 6 3 2

On (1) North bids Two Diamonds, not forcing, and on (2) he raises to Three Spades. Partner will know that the raise is defensive.

After the same sequence North holds:

   (3) ♠ 5   (4) ♠ Q 9 4 2
       ♡ K 10 6 4   ♡ 5
       ◇ A 9 7 5 3   ◇ A J 7 3
       ♣ K J 7   ♣ K 5 4 2

On (3) North redoubles, despite the singleton spade. It is most unlikely that the opponents will choose to defend against One Spade redoubled. Whatever they bid, North–South can double for penalties. On (4) the natural course is to redouble and follow with a raise to Three Spades. It is worth remarking, however, that many players treat 2NT in this sequence as equivalent to a sound, as opposed to a defensive, double raise. The logic of this convention is that with a fair, balanced hand, worth a normal 2NT, third hand can always redouble. When this convention is played, a redouble is always penalty-oriented.

Some special situations

In this section I comment briefly on some situations that often occur but do not call for long analysis.

Doubling after a pass

A player who has passed originally is free to double with less than would be expected in other circumstances. The bidding goes:

South	West	North	East
No	No	1S	No
2C	?		

West holds:

♠ 5 3
♡ K Q 5 4
♢ A J 7 4 2
♣ 3 2

West can safely double, indicating that he has values in the unbid suits.

Doubling in fourth position

The bidding goes:

South	West	North	East
1H	No	No	?

East holds:

♠ K 7 4 3
♡ 5
♢ Q J 8 6 4
♣ A 7 5

This is a minimum double in the protective position. With a slightly weaker hand the fourth player should reopen, if at all, with a suit bid rather than a double.

Double of opening Three bids

There are many systems of defence against an opening Three bid by an opponent. Most good players are content to play what is sometimes called an 'optional double' but is really a take-out double. Say that South opens Three Hearts as dealer. Now a double by West is primarily for take-out, 3NT is 'to play'.

SOS redoubles

A player who has been doubled in a part-score contract and who expects to make it should normally be happy to pass. In many situations, therefore, a redouble is used as a rescue manoeuvre.

South	West	North	East
1H	1S	dble	No
No	redble		

West has overcalled in a moderate suit and invites his partner to try a different suit or possibly 1NT.

South	West	North	East
1D	1S	dble	1NT
dble	No	No	redble

East does not propose to play in 1NT doubled or redoubled. He is asking West to try another suit; diamonds are not excluded.

Test of take-out doubles and responses

At game all, South opens One Diamond. As West, what action do you take on the following hands?

1 ♠ Q 10 7 5 3   2 ♠ K 2   3 ♠ K J 8 6 4
  ♡ K 9 6 4   ♡ A K 10 8 6 3   ♡ A Q 10 7 5 2
  ◇ —   ◇ 5   ◇ 4
  ♣ K J 8 3   ♣ A K 7 4   ♣ Q

Answers

1 Pass. You are well prepared for any suit response, it is true, but you would be unhappy if partner were to pass 1D doubled or were to respond in notrumps.

2 Double. If partner bids spades you can take out into hearts. The general strength is above the limit for a jump overcall of 2H.

3 1S. A double is seldom the best move on a two-suiters weak or strong. The bidding will develop more easily if you overcall in the higher-ranking of adjacent suits.

At love all the bidding begins:

South	West	North	East
1H	dble	redble	?

As East, what action do you take on the following hands?

1	♠ J 6 4	2	♠ 9 6	3	♠ K 10 8
	♡ 10 5 3		♡ J 7 4 2		♡ 8 6 4
	◇ Q 5 4 2		◇ 8 5		◇ Q J 7 5
	♣ 8 4 3		♣ J 8 6 4 3		♣ Q 8 4

Answers

1 Pass. You are under no obligation to bid on bad hands.

2 2C. Although you are not obliged to bid on bad hands, it is sometimes advisable to do so. Here at least you have a five-card suit and one effect of passing might be that partner would take out the redouble into 2D. A more subtle point is that if you allow partner to rescue himself into 1S, and this is doubled, the opponents will certainly double any further venture.

3 Pass. You have more than could be expected after an opening bid, a double and a redouble, but nothing is gained by bidding at this point.

At love all the bidding begins:

South	West	North	East
1D	dble	?	

As North, what action do you take on the following hands?

1	♠ A J 8 5	2	♠ K 10 5	3	♠ 5 3 2
	♡ K 4 2		♡ J 9 4		♡ Q 9 6 4
	◇ 8 5		◇ A 7 4		◇ K 8 7 5 2
	♣ 9 7 6 2		♣ J 7 6 2		♣ 4

Answers

1 Pass. There is no advantage in mentioning the moderate spade suit. For one thing, the opponents may bid this suit themselves.

2 1NT. You are not quite strong enough to redouble. By showing values at this level you may enable your partner to contest the part score in diamonds or clubs.

3 3D. Starting at the Three level, the opponents may not succeed in finding their best spot. Remember that the raise, after the double, is pre-emptive.

14

Stratagems in Play

The reader who has made a close study of the last few chapters may feel that his knowledge of bidding has outrun his knowledge of play. In a way, that is inevitable. It is possible to become reasonably proficient in bidding in quite a short time. Play is another matter. The field is so wide that it is possible only to plant a few general ideas. For the rest, there is no substitute for experience, preferably in a game with better players. In this chapter I describe some stratagems that occur in innumerable variations.

Hold-up play

The commonest of all manoeuvres by the declarer in a notrump contract is the *hold-up*. By holding up a winner to the second or third round, you hope to destroy communications between the defending hands. (See diagram p. 115.)

If playing the Stayman convention, North might respond Two Clubs, to discover whether his partner held four hearts. The final contract would be the same.

West leads the Queen of spades, top of a sequence. If East held K x alone he would unblock by covering with the King. With K 9 x he will play the 9 to show encouragement. To make it more difficult for the opponents to run their spade suit, South must hold up the Ace. West follows with the 8 of spades to East's King. South holds up again but has to win the third round.

Dealer, South   *Love all*

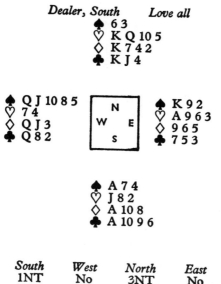

	South	West	North	East
	1NT	No	3NT	No
	No	No		

The hearts must be cleared now, for South will hardly make the contract without the tricks that can be established in hearts. If West holds the Ace of hearts with his five spades, nothing can be done.

It will make no great difference here, but East, on general principles, should in turn hold up the Ace of hearts until the third round. At this point he has no spade to play and will probably *exit* with the fourth heart or with a diamond.

South has eight tricks on top now – three hearts, two diamonds, two clubs and one spade. He knows that West is the danger hand, so for his ninth trick he runs the 10 of clubs, giving West no chance to obtain the lead. When the finesse holds, he takes it again and makes ten tricks.

It is often essential to hold up when you hold two winners in the suit led. This is a standard example:

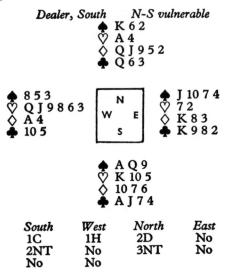

Dealer, South   *N-S vulnerable*

	♠ K 6 2	
	♡ A 4	
	◇ Q J 9 5 2	
	♣ Q 6 3	

♠ 8 5 3		♠ J 10 7 4
♡ Q J 9 8 6 3	N	♡ 7 2
◇ A 4	W E	◇ K 8 3
♣ 10 5	S	♣ K 9 8 2

	♠ A Q 9	
	♡ K 10 5	
	◇ 10 7 6	
	♣ A J 7 4	

South	West	North	East
1C	1H	2D	No
2NT	No	3NT	No
No	No		

West leads the Queen of hearts. Since he has a double *stop* in hearts, and a possibility even of a third trick, South may be tempted to win with the Ace of hearts in dummy and attack diamonds. This line would be good enough in an average game, but an expert player in East's position would protect his partner's entry by going up with the King of diamonds on the first round and clearing the hearts while West still had the Ace of diamonds.

South makes the contract quite easily so long as he plays low from both hands on the opening lead. Realising that his heart suit is probably dead, West may try a spade at trick 2, but South is too strong. He can establish the diamonds and make nine tricks with three spades, two hearts, three diamonds and the Ace of clubs. In most variations it will be safe to finesse the Jack of clubs for an overtrick.

Ducking

We remarked early on that a declarer with a holding such as K x x x opposite A x x would often duck the first or second round when aiming to establish the fourth round. This type of play is often made for entry reasons.

Dealer, North   *Love all*

```
              ♠ A 5
              ♡ J 10 3
              ◇ A K Q 5 2
              ♣ 6 4 2
♠ J 10 9 6 4   ┌─────────┐   ♠ K 8 2
♡ K 7          │    N    │   ♡ Q 9 5 4
◇ 8 3          │ W     E │   ◇ J 10 7 4
♣ Q 10 8 3     │    S    │   ♣ J 9
              └─────────┘
              ♠ Q 7 3
              ♡ A 8 6 2
              ◇ 9 6
              ♣ A K 7 5
```

South	*West*	*North*	*East*
—	—	1D	No
1H	No	2H	No
2NT	No	3NT	No
No	No		

West leads the Jack of spades. South plays low from dummy, East wins with the King and returns a spade.

Declarer can count, outside the diamonds, two tricks in spades, one in hearts, and two in clubs. He will therefore need four tricks from diamonds. Since the defence has knocked out the side entry, it would be dangerous to play off the top diamonds; if the suit failed to break 3–3 South would be cut off from the long diamond. The best play is to duck the first round of the suit. This will cost a trick if diamonds are 3–3, but declarer ensures the contract when the break is not worse than 4–2. A slight change in the diagram raises another point:

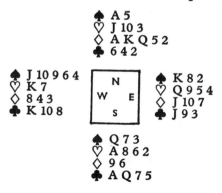

```
              ♠ A 5
              ♡ J 10 3
              ◇ A K Q 5 2
              ♣ 6 4 2
♠ J 10 9 6 4   ┌─────────┐   ♠ K 8 2
♡ K 7          │    N    │   ♡ Q 9 5 4
◇ 8 4 3        │ W     E │   ◇ J 10 7
♣ K 10 8       │    S    │   ♣ J 9 3
              └─────────┘
              ♠ Q 7 3
              ♡ A 8 6 2
              ◇ 9 6
              ♣ A Q 7 5
```

Again the contract is 3NT and the defence begins with a spade to the King and a spade back.

The difference now is that South has only A Q in clubs instead of A K. If he ducks a diamond he will have only eight certain tricks. Do you see how he can combine his chances? At Trick 3 he should finesse the Queen of clubs. If the finesse holds, he makes the safety play in diamonds, ducking the first round. If the finesse loses, as in the diagram, he wins the spade return and plays off the top diamonds, hoping for a 3–3 break.

Control in a suit contract

In suit contracts it is often very important to retain *trump control*. This means that you want to be able to draw the opposing trumps so that you can run off winners in a side suit. The examples that follow show two ways of retaining control.

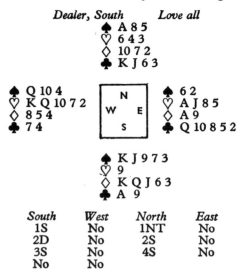

Dealer, South   *Love all*

♠ A 8 5
♡ 6 4 3
♢ 10 7 2
♣ K J 6 3

♠ Q 10 4
♡ K Q 10 7 2
♢ 8 5 4
♣ 7 4

♠ 6 2
♡ A J 8 5
♢ A 9
♣ Q 10 8 5 2

♠ K J 9 7 3
♡ 9
♢ K Q J 6 3
♣ A 9

South	West	North	East
1S	No	1NT	No
2D	No	2S	No
3S	No	4S	No
No	No		

West leads the King of hearts and follows with a low heart to the Ace, which South ruffs. South leads a spade to the Ace and returns a spade, to which East follows.

With eight cards, missing the Queen, the finesse is a better chance than the play for the drop, but on this occasion South must think about control. Supppose, first, that he finesses the Jack of spades. West wins in this position:

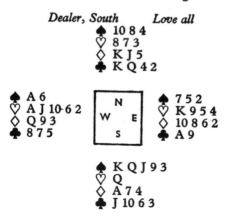

It is obvious that another heart from West will defeat the contract. If South ruffs and draws the outstanding trump he will have no protection against heart leads when East comes in with the Ace of diamonds.

Because of this danger, South should play the King of spades on the second round and clear the diamonds. This way, he loses just one spade, one heart and one diamond.

On the preceding deal South was obliged to ruff the hearts each time because he could not afford to lose a second trick in the suit. Sometimes the way to retain trump control is to decline to ruff until dummy can take care of the dangerous suit.

South	West	North	East
1S	No	1NT	No
No	2H	2S	3H
3S	No	No	No

After a typical part-score battle, South becomes the declarer in Three Spades. West begins with Ace of hearts and South ruffs the second round. West wins the second round of trumps and leads a third heart.

If South ruffs again, he can draw the outstanding trump but will be wide open when he loses to the Ace of clubs. The solution, in Three Spades, is to discard a diamond on the third round of hearts. The position will then be:

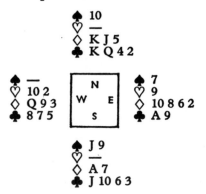

South has lost three tricks, but now he will lose only to the Ace of clubs. If East, who has the lead, plays another heart, South can take the force in dummy, so retaining trump control.

Declarer could also succeed, as the cards lie, if he ruffed the third heart and played on clubs before drawing the trump. This is an inferior line because of the danger of a club ruff.

15

Leads and Signals

It is customary to draw a distinction between declarer's play and defensive play, but really they are just different aspects of the same procedure. The mechanics of play are the same for both sides. All the stratagems we have described, such as finessing, hold-up play, ducking, and so forth, are used by the defenders as much as by the declarer. The play tends to *look* different because a defender sees the hand of an opponent, the dummy, not of his partner. Defence, in general, is more difficult, because it calls for imaginative reconstruction of partner's hand.

In this chapter we concern ourselves mostly with the ways in which the defenders communicate with one another by means of various signals. The process begins with the opening lead.

The lead at notrumps

The opening lead is an advantage because it enables the defenders to develop their own long suits before the declarer can start on his best suit. The opening leader will normally begin with his longest suit, but the primary objective, remember, is to develop the longest suit held by the partnership. In many cases it is better to study partner's hand rather than your own. Assume, in the following examples, that the bidding has been uninformative – just 1NT–3NT.

(1)   ♠ K J 7 4 2   (2)   ♠ A Q 6 4
        ♡ Q 6 3   ♡ Q 8 5
        ◇ 10 9   ◇ J 7 2
        ♣ J 7 3   ♣ 7 4 3

With (1) you must attack the spades, despite the possibility that you will be giving away a trick in the suit. The conventional card to lead is the fourth best, the 4.

The second hand is difficult. A spade certainly does not appeal from A Q x x. Many players would lead a club, choosing the 7. This might turn out well, but there are two reasons why a heart is slightly superior. The first is that opponents often have a concealed minor suit but seldom a concealed major. The second is that, leading a heart, you may achieve a positive result when partner holds something like K J 10 x or K J x x x . When you lead a club, you are just stalling, hoping not to give a trick away. Oddly enough, if the bidding had been more tentative, such as 1NT–2NT–3NT, there would be a stronger case for making the safe lead on what is likely to be a borderline contract. If you choose a heart or a diamond on this hand, begin with the low card, not the honour.

Again, after 1NT–3NT, you hold:

(3) ♠ 8 4   (4) ♠ 9 7 5 4 3
    ♡ Q J 10 6   ♡ 6 5 3
    ◇ K 9 6 4 2   ◇ J 7 4
    ♣ 9 3   ♣ Q 5

The hearts in (3) are so much better than the diamonds that you should certainly begin with the Queen of hearts. Hand (4) is so weak that it can hardly be right to lead a spade. You must play for your partner's hand. On the whole, the 6 of hearts represents the best chance. To lead the Queen of clubs, hazarding the only card in your hand that might take a trick, would be a somewhat desperate stroke.

It is normal, as you will have observed, to lead the top card from a solid or broken sequence such as Q J 10 or Q J 9 or K Q 10. When you hold an interior sequence such as A J 10 or Q 10 9, the traditional card is the middle honour, but from a five-card suit, when partner may hold a doubleton, fourth best will often turn out better.

The lead when partner has bid

'When in doubt, lead partner's suit' is a sound maxim. However, you must distinguish between an opening bid in a minor, which may represent a negligible holding, and an overcall, which must be based on a reasonably good suit. It is extremely annoying to suggest a lead and hear partner say at the end of the hand, 'I couldn't lead your suit because they bid notrumps over it.'

When leading partner's suit, lead low from three or four to an honour, the higher of touching honours, the top card from a doubleton. From three small, such as 8 5 2, the bottom card is best with an intelligent partner, who will be able to work out whether the 2 is a singleton or the lowest of three.

The lead in a suit contract

When leading against a suit contract, review the bidding and ask yourself: 'What type of hand is it?' Will declarer be drawing trumps? Is it necessary to attack or is a safe lead indicated?

Safe leads
When no suit has been mentioned other than the trump suit, in an auction such as 1S–2NT–4S, safety is an important consideration. You must aim to avoid giving a trick away. If you have no strong combination of honours, lead from a doubleton or three small, or even an innocuous trump. Make the declarer do his own work.

Attacking leads
When it looks as though the declarer may be making use of a long suit in dummy, you must aim to establish quick tricks for your own side. For example, the bidding goes:

South	West	North	East
1S	No	2H	No
2NT	No	3S	No
4S	No	No	No

Sitting West, you hold:

♠ 7 4
♡ Q 8 5
♢ K 10 6 4
♣ A 8 4 3

There will probably be a five-card heart suit in dummy and your holding of Q x x is unfavourable. You must certainly attack with a diamond or a club. If you decided to lead a club, the Ace would be better than a low one, but the obvious choice here is the 4 of diamonds.

Sometimes you must be still bolder. The bidding goes:

South	West	North	East
—	—	1C	No
1H	No	2C	No
3H	No	4H	No
No	No		

As West, you hold:

♠ K 5
♡ 7 3 2
♢ 10 9 7 5 4 2
♣ J 6

A diamond would be safe, but there is only one lead worth considering – the King of spades.

Short suit leads

The lead from a doubleton, still more of a singleton, will seldom cost a trick and may lead to a ruff. A lead from a short suit is especially promising when you hold a trick in the trump suit, such as A x or K x x. But never lead a singleton into declarer's side suit; you give away the distribution and may well kill a promising holding in your partner's hand.

Trump leads

A trump lead may be indicated when you can judge from the bidding that the declarer will be ruffing a side suit in dummy. The bidding goes:

South	West	North	East
1H	No	2D	No
2S	No	4S	No
No	No		

As West, you hold:

♠ 5 4 2
♡ 10 4
♢ A 6 3
♣ K Q 7 5 3

You have a strong holding in the unbid suit, clubs, but with four trumps in each hand the declarer will not mind being forced to ruff. A trump is indicated because South will be planning either to establish his hearts by ruffing in dummy or to play on crossruff lines. The best defence, probably, will be to lead trumps at every opportunity.

Forcing leads

There is not, as a rule, much point in leading from length, but this may be the right game when you hold four trumps (or when you can place your partner with length in trumps). The bidding goes:

South	West	North	East
1S	No	2C	No
2H	No	3S	No
4S	No	No	No

You have to lead from:

♠ 10 7 4 2
♡ A 6
♢ K J 7 4 3
♣ 5 3

Since you hold four spades, declarer may have difficulty in retaining trump control. You must attempt to weaken him by reading your long suit, diamonds. A forcing game is always an effective defence.

A question of tactics

Many writers on the game set out a 'table of preferred leads', with such estimable characters as A K Q and K Q J at the top of the list, and desperadoes such as A Q x and K x x at the bottom. This is the wrong approach; to make good leads against suit contract, you need to take a broader view.

Signals to show length and strength

There are many small ways in which the defenders can convey information to one another. We have seen, for example, that it is normal to lead the top card from a sequence; but when partner has led the suit it is correct to *play* the lowest card. The logic of this arrangement can be seen in this diagram:

```
              North
              10 6 4
   West                 East
   K 9 7 5 2            Q J 3
              South
              A 8
```

Defending against a suit contract, West leads the 5, East plays the Jack, and South wins with the Ace. Since the declarer, with A Q, would presumably have won with the Queen, West can place his partner with this card and may wish to underlead the King on the next round of the suit. If East had played the Queen and South had won with the Ace, West would have known nothing about the position of the Jack. Similarly, if East, from a holding such as Q 8 3, plays the Queen, West knows that declarer holds the Jack.

Signalling high-low

An unnecessarily high card normally denotes encouragement. A card such as the 7 from K J 7 4 2 may be played either when partner has led the Ace or when discarding on a different suit.

To play high-low, known as an *echo* or *peter*, signifies encouragement or, when there is no possibility of high cards, an even number. This is a very common situation in a suit contract:

```
              North
              Q 7 4
   West                 East
   A K 8 5 3            10 6
              South
              J 9 2
```

Since the normal lead from K Q is the King, many players lead the Ace from A K. Whichever card is led, East, holding a doubleton, drops the 10 and West knows that he can continue the suit and give his partner a ruff.

It should be added that among experienced players East would also drop a high card from four in this kind of position:

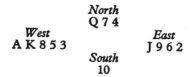

North
Q 7 4

West
A K 8 5 3

East
J 9 6 2

South
10

On the lead of the King (or Ace) East, holding an even number, plays the 9. It will usually be quite easy for West to judge that declarer holds a singleton and not three cards. When this understanding exists, East, with J 9 2, will play the 2, and West will read him for an odd number.

Good players use these distributional signals all the time to help their partners to count the hand. This is particularly important when the declarer is seeking to win tricks in a long suit held by the dummy. Suppose that this is a side suit:

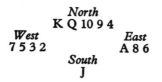

North
K Q 10 9 4

West
7 5 3 2

East
A 8 6

South
J

South leads the Jack and covers with dummy's Queen. With three cards West would play his lowest; with two or four he would play high-low. On the present occasion he plays the 5 and East will not make the mistake of ducking.

The same sort of situation often occurs in notrump contracts.

Dealer, South   *Game all*

♠ K Q J 9 3
♡ K 7 4
◇ 8 2
♣ Q 10 4

♠ 10 6 4
♡ 9 8
◇ 9 7 4 3
♣ K 8 3 2

N
W   E
S

♠ A 7 2
♡ A J 10 6 5
◇ J 5
♣ J 9 7

♠ 8 5
♡ Q 3 2
◇ A K Q 10 6
♣ A 6 5

South	West	North	East
1D	No	1S	No
1NT	No	2NT	No
3NT	No	No	No

Holding a poor hand, West plays for his partner and leads the 9 of hearts. Dummy plays low, East the 10 and declarer the Queen.

South leads the 5 of spades to the Jack and follows with the King. East, having seen his partner's 4 on the first round, knows that it is safe to win – or at any rate, that it cannot gain to hold up the Ace again. East switches to a club and South cannot take more than eight tricks.

Glossary of Bridge Terms and Phrases

(This glossary is confined to terms mentioned in the present book.)

Above the line	All scores other than those for tricks bid and made belong technically above the line that is drawn across the centre of the scoresheet.
Balance	To reopen the bidding after two passes, on the assumption that partner holds values.
Balanced	A balanced hand is one containing no short suits, usually 4–4–3–2, 4–3–3–3 or 5–3–3–2.
Below the line	Scores for tricks bid and made, such as 90 for Three Hearts, are entered below the centre line on the scoresheet.
Bid	Strictly, an undertaking to make a specified number of tricks; used also in respect of other calls.
Blackwood	A convention in which partner is asked to declare the number of Aces (and sometimes Kings) that he holds.
Call	A term covering any bid, pass, double, or redouble.
Clear	To clear a suit is to drive out winners held by the opponents.
Combination finesse	A finesse where two adjacent cards are missing, such as in A J 10.

Communication	The ability to go from hand to hand.
Contract	The final call establishes the contract in which the hand is played, either undoubled, doubled, or redoubled.
Control	An Ace or void represents first-round control of a suit, King or singleton second-round control. A declarer is said to lose trump control when he is unable to draw the opposing trumps and make his winners in the side suits.
Convention	An agreement by partners to use a bid or play in a sense not obvious on the surface.
Crossruff	The declarer is said to play a crossruff when he takes ruffs in the two hands alternately.
Cue bid	A bid that shows a control rather than a biddable suit; also, a bid of the opponent's suit.
Cut	The draw for partners; also, the dividing of the pack before the deal.
Declarer	The player who first named the denomination of the final contract (a suit or notrumps) and who in the play handles dummy's cards as well as his own.
Defender	In the bidding, a player of the side that did not open the bidding; in the play, an opponent of the declarer.
Denomination	A particular suit or notrumps.
Discard	The play of a card (not a trump) not belonging to the suit led.
Distribution	The pattern of suit-lengths in a player's hand; also, the division of a suit round the table.
Double	A call that increases the penalties if a contract is not made, and also the bonuses if it is made.

Double finesse	A finesse that seeks to entrap two cards, as when the 10 is finessed from A Q 10.
Double raise	A raise that covers two steps, as from One Heart to Three Hearts.
Doubleton	A holding of two cards.
Drop	Declarer plays for the drop when he plays top cards in preference to finessing.
Dummy	The partner of the declarer; his hand, which is exposed after the opening lead.
Echo	The play of a high card followed by a low card, as a signal.
Entry	A winner that affords entry to a player's hand.
Exit	To surrender the lead by playing a particular card.
Finesse	An attempt to win a trick with a card not the highest, taking advantage of the positional element in play.
Force	In bidding, to make a bid that is forcing for one round or forcing to game; in play, to force the declarer to ruff.
Game	A side that scores 100 below the line scores game. Two games by the same side win the rubber.
Grand slam	A contract to win all thirteen tricks.
Guard	A high card representing a 'stop' in an opponent's suit.
Hold-up	The refusal to part with a winning card.
Honour	An Ace, King, Queen, Jack, or 10.
Intervening bid	A bid by the defending side.
Jump	A jump bid, raise, response, or rebid, is a bid one range higher than necessary. A

jump overcall is a suit bid by the defending side, one range higher than necessary. Jump preference is a return to partner's suit one level higher than necessary.

Lead	The first card played to a trick is the lead. The opening lead is made by the player on the left of the declarer, subsequent leads by the player who won the previous trick.
Lightner double	A double of a freely bid slam contract, requesting an unexpected lead.
Major suit	Spades and hearts; Four of a major produces game.
Minor suit	Diamonds and clubs; Five of a minor produces game.
Negative response	The weakness response to a conventional bid.
No Bid	Call indicating a pass.
Notrumps	Denomination in which there is no trump suit.
Open	To make the first bid; to make the opening lead.
Overbid	A bid that exaggerates the value of the hand.
Overcall	Usually an intervening bid by a defender, especially by second hand over the opening bid.
Overruff	The play of a trump higher than that of a player who has already ruffed.
Overtrick	A trick in excess of the contract.
Part score	A contract scoring less than 100 below the line.
Pass	Call indicating that the player does not wish to bid, double, or redouble; usually expressed by the words, 'No bid'.

Penalty	Points scored above the line by the opponents of a player who has failed in his contract.
Penalty double	A double intended to penalise the opponents (as opposed to a take-out double).
Penalty pass	The pass of a take-out double, converting it into a penalty double.
Peter	The play of a high card followed by a low card, as a signal.
Plain suit	A suit other than the trump suit.
Point count	A method of valuation in which points are assigned to Aces, Kings, Queens, and Jacks.
Positive response	A response to a conventional bid, promising certain values (as opposed to a negative response).
Pre-empt	To make a high call with the object of buying the contract before the opponents have been able to exchange information.
Preference bid	A bid, or pass, expressing preference for one of two suits named by partner.
Preparedness	Choosing a bid that anticipates any response by partner.
Protect	To reopen the bidding after two passes, taking into account that partner probably holds good values.
Raise	Direct support for partner's bid.
Rebid	The second bid by a player, usually the opener; to repeat the denomination of a previous bid.
Redouble	A player who has been doubled may redouble, increasing the penalty if the contract fails, the bonus if it succeeds.

Responder	Initially, the partner of the opening bidder; the player who responds to any specific call.
Reverse	A player reverses when his second suit, bid at the Two level, is higher-ranking than his first suit, as in the sequence 1H–1NT–2S.
Revoke	Failure to follow suit when able to do so.
Rubber	The rubber, terminating the present period of play, is won by the first side to score two games.
Ruff	To play a trump when a plain suit has been led.
Ruffing finesse	The lead of equal cards when a higher card played by second hand can be ruffed.
Sacrifice	A bid likely to incur a penalty, made to save a game or slam.
Save	Deliberately invite a penalty, to prevent opponents from scoring a game or slam.
Sequence	A group of consecutive cards, such as K Q J. K Q 10 is a broken sequence, K 10 9 an interior sequence.
Show out	Fail to follow suit, having none of the suit led.
Shut-out	A bid designed to prevent the opponents from exchanging information; similar to pre-empt.
Side suit	A suit other than the trump suit; same as plain suit.
Simple overcall, preference, raise, rebid, response	One made at minimum level.
Single raise	Usually a raise from One to Two.
Singleton	The holding of one card in a suit.

Slam	Contract to make twelve or thirteen tricks.
Small slam	Contract to make twelve tricks.
SOS redouble	A redouble that asks partner to rescue into another denomination.
Stayman	A convention whereby a player who has opened 1NT (or 2NT) is requested to name a four-card major.
Stop	The holding of a high card that will prevent an opponent from running a suit at notrumps.
Support	To raise partner's bid; trump support is the holding in a suit called by partner.
Take-out	The bid of a new suit, such as 2D over 1H or over 1NT.
Take-out double	A double that seeks information from partner and is not intended as a penalty double.
Throw-in	This occurs when all four players have passed.
Trick	The unit of play, consisting of four cards, one from each player.
Trump	A suit, named in the bidding, that in the final contract has superior rank to the others (subject to the obligation to follow suit).
Trump control	When declarer can draw trumps and retain the lead, so that he can make his winners in the side suits, he has trump control.
Unblock	The play of a card that might block the run of a suit or prevent a convenient entry or win an unwanted trick.
Underbid	A bid that understates a player's values. (A bid not high enough to overcall a previous bid is an insufficient bid.)

Undertrick   The trick or tricks by which declarer falls short of his contract.

Void   To have no cards of a suit.

Vulnerable   A side that has won a game is vulnerable, after which penalties and some bonuses are increased.

Index

Most entries refer to the first occasion on which a term or subject is mentioned.

above the line   14
Acol system   80
auction bridge   9

below the line   14
Blackwood convention   92
bonus for doubled contract   95

call   6
contract   5
control   91
  in play   118
convention   32
crossruff   44
cue bid   91
Culbertson system   81
cut for deal   9
cut for partners   9

deal   9
declarer   9
discard   3
double   6
  for take-out   103
  of INT   106
  of Three bids   111
double raise   60
ducking   25, 116
dummy   9

echo   126
entry cards   18

finesse   21–3
force   56, 62
  in play   125
forcing two   81

game   7
grand slam   8, 89

hold-up play   115
honours   1, 95

intermediates   37
intervention   64

jump overcall   99
jump preference   78
jump responses   62

lead   9, 21
lightner double   107

major suit   5
minor suit   5
misdeal   9

negative response   80
notrump bidding   35
notrumps   5

open   6, 52
opener's rebids   68
opening 3NT   87
optional double   111

overcall 7, 97, 99
overruff 4
overtrick 11, 94

part score 7, 65
pass 6
penalty 6, 96
penalty double 103
penalty pass 104
Peter 126
point count 35
positive response 81
pre-emptive bidding 84
protecting 99

raise 7
  of INT 38
  of suit bid 57, 60, 62
rebids by INT opener 40
  by suit opener 68
redouble 6
  for rescue 112
responding
  after a pass 63
  over intervention 74
  to overcalls 100
  to Three bids 86
responses
  to INT 35

to suit bids 56–61
reverse bid 73
revoke 14
rubber 7
  unfinished 95
ruff 4, 42–3
ruffing finesse 49

sacrifice 7
signalling 125–8
slam 8, 89–93
Stayman convention 39, 80

Three notrump opening 87
throw-in 6
trial bid 76
trick 2
trumps 3
Two bids 80
Two notrump opening 80

unblock 50
undertricks 96

vulnerable 15

weak Two bids 80